THE PROGRESSIVE'S POCKETBOOK OF PERSUASION

A TOOLKIT FOR REACHING AMERICAN VOTERS

BY:

COURTNEY DILLARD, Ph. D.

Note for Librarians: A cataloguing record for this book is available from Library and Archives Canada at www.collectionscanada.ca/amicus/index-e.html

ISBN 1-4120-9491-7

Printed in Victoria, BC, Canada. Printed on paper with minimum 30% recycled fibre.
Trafford's print shop runs on "green energy" from solar, wind and other environmentally-friendly power sources.

TRAFFORD
PUBLISHING™
Offices in Canada, USA, Ireland and UK

Book sales for North America and international:
Trafford Publishing, 6E–2333 Government St.,
Victoria, BC V8T 4P4 CANADA
phone 250 383 6864 (toll-free 1 888 232 4444)
fax 250 383 6804; email to orders@trafford.com
Book sales in Europe:
Trafford Publishing (UK) Limited, 9 Park End Street, 2nd Floor
Oxford, UK OX1 1HH UNITED KINGDOM
phone 44 (0)1865 722 113 (local rate 0845 230 9601)
facsimile 44 (0)1865 722 868; info.uk@trafford.com
Order online at:
trafford.com/06-1246

10 9 8 7 6 5 4 3 2

Dedicated to: All the good people who keep fighting the hard fight

TABLE OF CONTENTS

NOTE TO READER

Thank you for picking up the Progressive's Pocketbook of Persuasion. This book rests on several assumptions you should be aware of. First, as a handbook of sorts, this book is designed for people who are interested in actively engaging in persuasion—it should be read AND used. Leafing through it, nodding at some of the suggestions, and putting it back up on the shelf will mean that the book has failed to serve its purpose. You need to spend some time with each chapter, wrestle with the suggestions, and try out the tools offered within these pages.

Second, while I acknowledge that Progressives approach politics from a wide variety of angles, this book assumes that most Progressives affiliate, at least to some degree, with the Democratic Party. Throughout the book I use the terms Progressive and Democrat interchangeably, while being aware they are not always the same thing. This is in part because at this juncture, I strongly believe that the aims of most Progressives can best be met through aligning with the Democrats and participating in the existing two-party system. At the same time, I am hopeful that in the future, once the Conservative trend in American politics has been clearly reversed, there will be a productive place for additional parties.

Third, I come from a background in persuasion theory that includes the study of classical persuasion or rhetoric. The early Greeks saw rhetoric as an important public art in which a person was able to discern the most effective means of persuasion in any given situation. As such, I use the term *rhetoric* here in the classical sense of persuasion and not in its more contemporary form which suggests empty language.

Fourth, while this book is primarily about Party politics, almost all of the tools highlighted in this handbook can be used

Note to Reader

by persuaders in broader contexts. As you read through the book, consider how you might apply the lessons learned here to other Progressive endeavors where persuasion is key, such as issue campaigns and grassroots organizing.

Lastly, the reader should recognize that this book offers only one piece of the puzzle. How we communicate with our fellow Americans is a critical factor in our future success; but in the end we will not win the day on words alone. We will also have to do the harder work of crafting innovative policies, training future political leaders, and offering Americans an authentic new vision they not only agree with, but are willing to work for.

INTRODUCTION

November 2nd, 2004–11:45 PM PST: We lost. There were no WMDs, the budget surplus was replaced by the largest deficit the country had ever seen, the economy was unstable with jobs being shipped overseas, and the Republican candidate was vulnerable to critique on many fronts. But we lost. And we didn't just lose the presidency. We lost seats in both the Senate and the House and aside from a few bright spots, faced defeat in State races across the country.

Depressing isn't it? Especially when we have smarter candidates and better policies. When we care deeply about the issues of the day, taking to the streets against the war, raising our voices in protest as jobs steadily flow out of the country, or looking for loopholes to the social service cuts the Republicans keep trying to pass. So many of us feel like we're fighting for average Americans, at the same time we are losing their votes. We were shocked by our losses on November 2nd and particularly by those voters who seemed to vote against their economic interests. Their votes made no sense. Following the election many Progressives shook our heads and asked – What's wrong with our fellow Americans? But now that the shock has worn off we must be brave enough to ask ourselves a much more difficult, but also more productive question: What is wrong with us?

And in asking that question we must be strong enough to accept the answer. We lost because we couldn't talk the talk. Our messages are out of line with the way everyday Americans think and make their decisions. Our values do not resonate. Our words do not inspire. Though we are still fighting for the average American, those same people often see Progressives as irrelevant, out of touch, or irresponsible. In essence, we lost the election because we have lost control of the conversation. As a result of this loss, we are forced to choose between two ineffective

1

approaches: echoing the messages of our opponents or proposing our own ideas at a time when they fall on deaf ears or are met with overt hostility.

This analysis is not new. Following the 2004 elections, pundits emerged from every corner of society to offer various diagnoses as to what was ailing the Democratic Party. Whether it was Thomas Frank's argument that Democrats did not understand the Republicans' brilliant hijacking of populism by rhetorically replacing issues of class with those of culture, Lakoff's work on framing, which explains how the Democrats have lost ground on influencing Americans' foundational values, or James Carville's succinct analysis that we are unable to craft compelling narratives–they all point in the same direction. We are losing the war because we have not effectively developed the crucial fighting power of persuasion.

Our lack of persuasive prowess is a serious problem, not just for us, but for the country and the larger world. The Republican Party is leading the country based on a disastrous formula. In essence, they tell the American people what they want to hear, all the while pursuing their own plans, many of which negatively impact those same Americans. They talk about security, while engaging in a war whose fallout will jeopardize the safety of Americans for decades to come. They speak about the persistence of the American Dream, as they pass legislation which insures that the wealthy stay that way and those at the bottom stay there as well. They talk about the importance of a limited government, while seeking to extend the government's reach into our private lives. And, they talk about fiscal responsibility, as they run up the largest deficit this country has ever seen. The Republicans' empty promises and harmful policies have real material consequences: instability in world affairs, erosion of respect on the international front, abandonment of our most vulnerable populations, and destruction of the Earth's resources are among them. While Republicans are winning over Americans with their words, they are eroding the infrastructure that offers those same Americans a decent life.

Introduction

Progressives need to step up to the plate. We need to get serious about persuasion and be ready to seize the political opportunity that is emerging. Recently, cracks have begun to appear in the Conservative's façade. Americans are growing tired ✗ of the fear appeals. They are casting wary eyes towards plans to rollback government across the board. They are unsatisfied. In this context, Progressives must be ready to respond.

There is a lot of work to be done. Our political leaders need to create innovative policy solutions. They need to present a united front more often. They need to be braver. But all of us, whether we voice our opinions at family gatherings, volunteer with our county or state parties, or run for office ourselves, must improve our persuasion. Every Progressive must be disciplined in learning and applying the tools of persuasion in the public sphere. This book is designed to help you do that. Each short chapter introduces a distinct tool of persuasion, explores how political persuaders have used it in the contemporary context, and provides specific ways you can utilize the tool in the future.

BEFORE YOU CAN GET STARTED

Progressives often have lots of ideas and most Progressives are eager to share them. They believe, as advocates generally do, that the power is in the idea itself. They assume that if it makes sense to them at a certain time, it will make sense to everyone at anytime. And yet, by now, each of us has caught glimpses of the fact that this might not be the case. In truth, ideas must be communicated in a complex process involving other people and outside conditions. The very WORST mistake you can make is to craft a persuasive appeal without considering the audience you are addressing and the context in which you are speaking. Before you can ever really persuade anyone, you need to take a long look around and assess these key variables.

3

Introduction

Audience

The two most important questions you should ask before you begin any attempt at persuasion are: *"Who is my audience?"* and *"What do they care about?"* Persuaders who craft their appeals with disregard for the audience who is receiving them are certain to be ineffective. In deciding the best audience for your appeal, you must determine who is likely to be persuaded by your message. All of us have a limited amount of time to participate in persuasion. It only makes sense that we would want to make the most of that time and address audiences that we might actually persuade. This eliminates two key audiences—those who staunchly oppose our message, and those who already agree with us. While this might make perfect sense on paper, each of us knows it is not so easy in practice. All too often, we end up wasting our energy on family members who have voted straight ticket Republican for 40 years or basking in the comfort of applause from like-minded Progressives at left-leaning political events. When we do this, we are violating one of the strictest rules in communication: don't waste time on the people who will never support you or the people who already do. Instead, we must concentrate our efforts on persuading people who sympathize with our message to be clear supporters and people who are open but skeptical of our message to at least sympathize with our cause. In essence, it is the middle that matters.

And just what type of person makes up the potential audience for Democrats? Of course, there has been a lot of research done to answer this important question. Key constituencies in the 2004 election included students, senior citizens, minorities (especially African-Americans and Hispanics), women, and union members. But we cannot count on these alone. After the results came in from the last election, we had to face the fact that students do not vote in large numbers even when they are registered, women can be won over by Republican fear appeals and the abortion issue, senior citizens are growing more conservative, and minorities or union members may care

4

more about cultural issues like gay marriage than they do about potential threats to their jobs.

The results of the 2004 election were our wake up call: Progressives must change a fundamental aspect of our persuasion. We need to replace our emphasis on difference with an emphasis on similarity. Instead of courting supporters by appealing to their particular interests, we need to see our audience first and foremost as Americans. In crafting our persuasion we must appeal to that which we all hold in common. Republicans already do this. Take the 2004 election. While we were making bumper stickers reading *Pacific Islanders for Kerry* and T-shirts emblazoned with *Teamsters for Kerry*, the Republicans created a simple *W* which could be displayed by all of their supporters.

While there can be no doubt that different audiences care about different things and may be influenced by different messages, there is also no doubt that at a deeper level some things are still held in common by most Americans. If there is one thread that runs through effective political persuasion, it is the ability to clearly appeal to that which is common amongst us, that which is shared. In essence, good persuaders start from shared ground in order to create appeals that resonate with their audience. They also use this safe jumping-off point to subsequently influence their audience's way of thinking, slowly working to change their assumptions at various levels.

In addition to assessing who might be most receptive to our message, we also need to try to broaden the audiences we have access to. Most Progressives feel comfortable talking politics in their social circle, but in order to really make a difference, each of us must be willing to spread the message further afield. We need to commit ourselves to proudly standing on the soapbox and actively reaching out to new audiences. Some forms of outreach available to every Progressive include writing letters to the editor, talking with your neighbors about key issues, becoming involved in peace and social justice committees in your faith community, hosting house parties around national events or on topics of state/local concern, and speaking to civic clubs or at political events. What matters is that each person takes responsibility for promoting the Progressive message whenever and wherever they can. As more and more Progressive voices speak clearly to their fellow Americans from values they hold in common and on topics of shared concern, more Americans will align with our vision. Voice by voice, we will begin to reclaim the common ground.

Context

Broad Cultural Trends

Effective political persuaders are always surveying the political landscape, trying to gauge whether the time is right to focus on a specific idea or advance a particular message. They keep an eye on broader social trends at the same time they evaluate particular contexts to in order to weigh the worth of their persuasive efforts. From a broad view, there are several key trends that have emerged in the last 25 years which Progressives need to be aware of. Some of these trends are the result of sophisticated strategies pursued by the Republican Party, while others can be traced to our own missteps or mistakes. In general, these trends set the backdrop for the contemporary picture and offer insight into why we find it so hard to effectively reach our fellow Americans.

The first trend is tied to the well-documented success of Ronald Reagan and his drive to make average Americans increasingly distrustful of the government and resentful of taxation. He rhetorically cultivated this perspective with the American public through the use of such famous phrases as "The nine most terrifying words in the English language are 'I'm from the government and I'm here to help'." While a suspicion of government has existed in various forms since the founding of our country, the success of Reagan's more contemporary message is quite evident as our society has formed an overarching consensus that government is the problem and not the solution. This assumption has made the persuasive work of Progressives very difficult. Most Progressives believe that a well-run

6

government can improve the lives of all Americans. They see government as the instrument of a civilized and just society. And they believe that taxation, particularly of the very wealthy, is a fair approach to funding that government. In the post Reagan era, Progressives have clearly floundered in their attempts to articulate the necessity of taxation and a positive role for government.

2. The second trend marks another rhetorical success on the part of Republicans. During the last few decades Republicans have used anti-tax messages and the persistent labeling of Democrats as elites to position themselves as the party of the people. In so doing, they have taken the Populist platform from our party. This move was facilitated by the working class' growing resentment towards certain groups of people: minority welfare recipients, radical college students and faculty, environmentalists, and the media, particularly the Hollywood elite. Republicans used that opportunity to create a Populism that reflects a more affluent working class and downplays economic differences while highlighting cultural ones. At the same time Republicans aligned with the interests of the average Americans, they also took every opportunity to portray Democrats as elites who were out of touch with those same Americans. This is done by consistently equating loose morals with liberal politics: casting Democrats as supporters of abortion, flag burning, and taxation, and opponents of the 10 Commandments, school prayer, and entrepreneurship. The Conservatives set the agenda and then measured us by it. Cast in such a light, Progressives clearly do not reflect the lives and values of the average American. In essence, Republicans seized the opportunity to characterize themselves as the representatives of the everyday American, and we let them.

3. The third important trend of note is the increasing influence of polling and focus groups in politics. Part of a larger trend of professionalizing the political sphere, these research tools have had an enormous impact on the way Democrats have reached out to the public. While there is no doubt that both parties follow polls and respond to them in various ways, there is an important distinction to be made. Even while using polling to

craft their messages, Republicans almost never waiver from their policies. Instead, they poll to find out how they can best sell those policies to the American people. Democrats, on the other hand, often poll to craft their messages *and* their policies. We listen too intently to pollsters who tell us to move to the middle and build policy solely from what the public is currently thinking. In essence, we lead by letting others tell us where to go. Progressives can learn something from the Republicans here. Sometimes leadership must involve shifting the public's perspective rather than responding to it. Persuasive appeals must be grounded in conviction or they will be empty and flat. If we do not believe in our message, we will not be passionate in our persuasion.

④ The last trend is the most complex and perhaps the most influential. Following WWII, postmodern thought spread throughout Europe and the United States. While defying simple definitions, the postmodern perspective is marked by a rejection of absolutes in favor of relativism, a dismissal of unification in favor of a pluralism based on individual interests, a move away from order towards the celebration of chaos, and the death of moral authority. Some Progressives, primarily academics, knowingly embraced this perspective hoping that it would give voice to those less powerful and help avoid the violence of Fascism. Most Progressives, however, became conditioned to this perspective as it emanated from various parts of the culture, particularly the media. While the relativism of postmodernism appeals to Progressives when it masquerades as tolerance, it has in many ways been our Trojan horse. Postmodernism appears to advance the public good by creating tolerance for a wide variety of views and lifestyles, but in the end that same tolerance robs us of the ethical basis for making political arguments. We are painted in shades of gray, appearing to hold no firm values. By embracing everything, we can judge nothing.

This is very politically problematic because despite the influx of postmodern thought, human beings continue to desire unity, authority, and meaning. In addition, economic reasoning fills the void left by the removal of moral argument with everyone arguing on behalf of his or her own economic interests. Republicans have found a nice balance in this climate, sometimes embracing moral language and sometimes taking an economic approach. Democrats have had trouble with both.

The Contemporary Landscape
These trends have converged to create the backdrop for our contemporary political landscape. Republicans have been very strategic in both furthering these trends and responding to them rhetorically. They speak the language the public wants to hear, even as their policies move in a very different direction. They continue to label the Democrats the party of tax and spend while they run up the largest deficit the country has ever had, and which our children will be forced to pay off. They align themselves with the interests of the everyday American while acting in the interest of the wealthy. They speak about independent leadership while taking direction from big business and the defense industry. They cloak themselves in religious language, while ignoring central tenents, such as Jesus' call to alleviate poverty. Finally, they claim the moral high ground while excusing all manner of unethical behavior from torture of prisoners to domestic spying, to campaign finance scandals.

And yet we catch glimpses that it's not too late for us to turn the tide. There are signs that Progressives could win back the hearts and minds of average Americans if they were able to effectively communicate their messages to that audience. The American people are showing signs of defection from the Conservatives' camp. They don't believe the government should go poking around in our private lives. They don't believe that our safety net should be so thin that we cannot help our own citizens in times of natural disaster. They don't believe that their political leaders should be exempt from an expectation of ethical behavior. And, they don't believe that our country can go on fighting the war in Iraq forever. All around us we see the tide of public opinion turning against the Republican agenda. And yet, it

9

would be foolish to think that the recent mistakes of the Republican Party were enough to guarantee election victories or could substitute for true leadership. Progressives desperately need to craft their own plans and make their own persuasive appeals.

In order to effectively step up to the plate, we need to bravely face the conditions of the contemporary context and the existing political climate. Many Progressives look to the 1960s, citing that era as a time when Progressive thought ruled the day. But looking backwards to a very different context will not provide much direction for the way forward. We cannot remain blind to the fact that much has changed in America in the last several decades. Some of these changes include the concentration of media ownership and its impact on the variety of messages communicated to the American public, the increase in affluence of America's working class, the growing influence of money in elections, the empowerment of women and their move away from minority status, globalization, the rise in conservative religious fundamentalism, the impact of the September 11th attacks and the resulting War on Terrorism. Progressives must speak from an understanding of the contemporary landscape in which we live.

Seizing Opportunity for the Future

Recognizing that the contemporary landscape is one in which Progressives must speak, and speak effectively, we must also evaluate the opportunity available in each specific context. Such an approach to persuasion requires a practical assessment of whether a particular time and place will allow the persuader to effectively convey his message. Too often Progressives ignore this advice and articulate their perspectives in ineffective contexts like Right wing radio programs where the host cuts them off every time they make a salient point or informal conversations where their listeners nod absent-mindedly but do not really absorb the message. Progressives need to find contexts where we can effectively explain our views. We also need to focus our attention on new contexts in which the right audiences are present.

In addition to evaluating the context around us, we must also rapidly respond to the political opportunities that it presents. In the past, Progressives were often slow to recognize and respond to situations we could have framed in our favor. A good example of this is found in John Kerry's slow response to the Swift Boat ads. Because Kerry did not respond immediately, his voice was not part of the equation whereby the American people evaluated the claims they were confronted with. Our hesitation has come from disorganization and disputes at various levels within the party structure, the fear that we would pay a price for speaking up, and just plain uncertainty at how best to respond. As a result, we have often lost valuable momentum and missed many political opportunities. Democrats need to think ahead and prepare our persuasion.

In sum, effective persuasion is built on accurate assessment of both audience and context. Progressives need to know who they want to talk to and the landscape in which they are making their appeal. An understanding of audience and context consistently influences the persuader's choice of what tools to use, as well as how to use them. If we want America to move forward, we must begin by discovering how Americans see themselves, what they value, and how they may be influenced by the current landscape they are living in. Keep these concepts in the forefront of your mind as you read this handbook.

CHAPTER 1

ABOVE THE FRAY OF THE CULTURE WAR

In the last decade or so there has been a lot of talk about culture wars. While pundits suggest a growing divide among Americans over what our culture should look like, a quick glance beneath the surface reveals that the American people have a lot more in common than we think. American culture (not just that represented by the books we read or the music we enjoy but the culture which serves as the grounding for our fundamental beliefs and values) creates and reinforces a truly unique American perspective. These distinct patterns and lessons are found deep in the fabric of our society and our individual identities. Even as those patterns change or voices from subcultures challenge American norms, traces still remain of that which binds each individual to American society.

Good persuaders recognize the power of culture. They know culture creates commonalities, and as a result becomes a vital ingredient in crafting effective persuasive appeals. Even persuaders who want to fundamentally alter the culture must find common ground before motivating their audience to consider change. Political persuaders, who typically approach their audience first and foremost as Americans, should be especially cognizant of the tenents of American culture. Cultural theorists have created several sets of lists which attempt to summarize the characteristics of American culture by exploring the persistent beliefs, values, and behaviors of the American people. As you read the lists below, note which components have become the rhetorical property of the Republicans, and which are more apt to be associated with Democrats.

Beliefs[1]

All of us have a set of beliefs, which essentially act as our perception of reality. We rely on these beliefs to tell us what is true or valid in the world and also to guide our decisions. While beliefs come from a variety of sources, they are most influenced by the society in which we live. In addition, after we have adopted specific beliefs, we often turn to sources within the culture to have those beliefs reinforced, while avoiding those sources that may challenge or try to change our beliefs. The following beliefs are prominent throughout American culture:

Primary beliefs:
- Everyone must work
- People must benefit from their work
- Manual labor is respectable

Immigrant beliefs:
- Improvement is possible
- Opportunities must be imagined
- Freedom of movement is needed for success

Frontier beliefs:
- You learn by doing
- Each person is responsible for his own well-being
- Helping others helps yourself
- Progress requires organization

Religious and moral beliefs:
- God created nature and human beings
- God created a law of right and wrong
- Doing what is right is necessary for happiness
- God gave every man the same birthrights
- America is a chosen country

---

[1] McElroy, 1999

Social beliefs:
- Society is a collection of individuals
- Every person's success improves society
- Achievement determines social rank

Political beliefs:
- The people are sovereign
- The least government possible is best
- A written constitution is essential to government
- A majority decides
- Worship is a matter of conscience

Beliefs on human nature:
- Almost all human beings want to do what is right
- Human beings will abuse power when they have it

Many of these beliefs have consistently served as the foundation for political persuasion in America. Good political persuaders work hard to place their favored beliefs at the forefront of American minds and then focus on them as they build their persuasive appeals. While both parties gesture to most of these beliefs at one time or another, each has tended to favor some over others.

In the last 25 years, Republican policies and perspectives have primarily reflected the cultural beliefs that *everyone must work, each person is responsible for his own well-being, society is a collection of individuals,* and *the least government possible is best.* They have also worked to associate themselves with the entire category of *religious and moral beliefs.* Democrats, on the other hand, are more likely to affiliate with beliefs like *people must benefit from their work, helping others helps yourself, every person's success improves society,* and *worship is a matter of conscience.* Democrats have also affiliated with the beliefs concerning *human nature.* While both sets of beliefs are available to use in creating effective persuasion, Republicans have been more vocal in articulating their set. As they hone in on particular cultural beliefs, others, most notably those held by Progressives, are overshadowed in the minds of many Americans.

There have been several political skirmishes over American beliefs in the last few years, but there are two key struggles worth looking at in greater detail. The first of these is over the belief that *the least government possible is best.* Because this is a belief that has typically hurt Democrats, Republicans continue to use it as part of their rhetorical arsenal, particularly during elections. During the 2000 election, Dick Cheney suggested that the Bush-Cheney ticket was the better option because it rejected "big government."

"This is a very important decision you're going to make on November 7. We have a fundamental choice between whether or not we continue with our old ways of big government, high taxes and ever more intrusive bureaucracy, or whether we take a new course for a new era."-Dick Cheney, October 5th, 2000

Four years later, President Bush relied on this same belief to cast doubt on Senator Kerry's health-care plan:

"He (Kerry) said he's going to have a novel health-care plan. You know what it is? The federal government is going to run it. It is the largest increase in federal government healthcare ever. And it fits with his philosophy . . That's what liberals do. They create government-sponsored healthcare. Maybe you think that make sense. I don't." -George Bush, October 8th, 2004

In some situations, Republicans pair big government with other policies or groups they dislike so that the American people will quickly reject them as is the case with comments by California Governor Arnold Schwarzenegger who backed initiatives to limit the collection and use of union dues:

"Big government unions should not use members' funds as a personal kitty....Union bosses have too much power over members' paychecks and too much power over our state." -Arnold Schwarzenegger, October 14th, 2005

While Republicans continue to rely upon this belief, the policies of the Neo-conservatives have given Democrats an important opportunity to use the belief in their favor. The concept of big government can be understood in two ways: more taxes for more services or more laws for greater restrictions. Contemporary conservatives, unlike their traditional counterparts, are interested in expanding laws and legislation which would reduce personal freedom. Some of the areas in which these laws might apply concern sexual relations between consenting adults, end of life decisions, and access to private communications. Progressives should work to change the perception of big government in terms of taxes and government agencies, to big government in terms of restrictive policies which intrude upon people's privacy or limit individual choice. In so doing, they could depend upon the commonly held belief that big government is bad, while slightly shifting how the American people understand what big government *is*. Below are some recent examples of this strategy:

"I believe that a woman has a right to make up her own mind about what kind of health care she gets, and I think Democrats believe that in general.... The issue is whether a woman has a right to make up her own mind about her health care, or a family has a right to make up their own mind about how their loved ones leave this world. I think the Republicans are intrusive and they invade people's personal privacy, and they don't have a right to do that."-Howard Dean, May 22nd, 2005

"I think first of all what's happening in the Schiavo case is a terrible tragedy. I mean, it's just painful to watch.... This is something that as a moral issue should be left to the family. .I think it is wrong to have a bunch of politicians in Washington getting involved in this." -John Edwards, March 30th, 2005

Strategic Progressives also recognize that context sometimes provides an opportunity for discussion over the appropriate level of government. Situations like the government's response to Hurricane Katrina and the flooding of New Orleans create the potential for conversations on the essential role of government in a civilized society. When media coverage turns its powerful spotlight on the lives of the American poor, when we see the costs of a government rendered impotent by cuts and carelessness, Progressives have the opportunity to make a case for the appropriate role of government. Most Americans believe that some government is needed in order for our society to function. This existing belief allows Progressives to subtly shift current discussions about government size to more productive discussions about government efficiency. Within this framework, Democrats can key on efficiency and organization at the same time they make the case for government's central role in specific aspects of our society.

The other contemporary struggle is over *religious and moral beliefs*. As was made all too clear in discussions following the 2004 election, Republicans have successfully positioned themselves as the party of values. As an oft-cited post-election poll revealed, a large majority of the values-driven voters voted for George Bush. In part, Republicans have become the party of values by limiting the discussion about ethics to a narrow set of concerns regarding religion in public life and sexual morality. The Clinton sex scandal, the Democrats association with abortion on demand, and other public debates around what our schools should teach and the media should display, have made it easy for Republicans to suggest Progressives lack values. In addition, Progressives have often hesitated to articulate their personal religious views or moral standards. In many ways, we've have been hampered by the plague of postmodernism referred to earlier. We do not want to express religious convictions because those convictions can be associated with intolerance. At the same time, we are unable to articulate a strong morality outside of religion because we cannot agree on the common ground it should come from. And yet, as poll after poll reveals, people want to know the moral and religious beliefs of their party and their potential representatives. In a time of uncertainty, the American people are looking for basic moral convictions they can rely on.

In the 2004 election, Kerry was correctly criticized for saying too little too late about his religious and moral beliefs. Not only did President Bush discuss his beliefs much more frequently than Kerry, he appeared comfortable discussing them, while Kerry seemed stilted and unnatural. Bush also tied his political decisions to his beliefs whenever possible. For example, during the 2004 debates when both candidates were confronted with questions about abortion, a top moral issue for many Americans, George Bush directly responded based on his beliefs:

"I think it's important to promote a culture of life. I think a hospitable society is a society where every being counts and every person matters. I believe the ideal world is one in which every child is protected in law and welcomed to life. I understand there are great differences on this issue of abortion. But I believe reasonable people can come together and put good law in place that will help reduce the number of abortions." -George Bush, October 8th, 2005

Kerry, on the other hand, had trouble articulating his convictions:

"I can't tell you how deeply I respect the belief about life and when it begins. But I cannot take what is an article of faith for me and legislate it for someone who doesn't share that article of faith…you have to afford people their constitutional rights. And that means being smart about allowing people to be fully educated. I think it's important for the United States, for instance, not to have this rigid ideological restriction on helping families around the world to be able to make a smart decision." -John Kerry, October 8th, 2005

Kerry was not the only Democrat during the 2004 election that was unable to articulate a clear moral position on specific issues. For example, when the *Florida Times-Union* asked Florida Senate candidates Betty Castor and Mel Martinez, "Should there be a constitutional amendment banning gay marriage? Why or why not?" Castor answered the question with a policy-oriented answer:

"I do not support gay marriage, but I oppose a change in the U.S. Constitution over this issue. We should be conservative with our Constitution, not change it over contentious social issues. I do support basic legal protections for couples who make a commitment to each other, such as the right to visit each other in the hospital." -Betty Castor

Mel Martinez, on the other hand, offered a simple answer that rested on his beliefs:

"I believe a marriage should be between a man and a woman." -Mel Martinez

What Progressives need is a strong foundation to confront the moral issues that are always part of the political equation in America. Religious Republicans have typically rested their beliefs upon a conservative interpretation of the Bible, often referencing the Old Testament and focusing on punishment for sexual immorality or disregard for God's laws. Non-religious Republicans rest their beliefs primarily on the tenets of free-market capitalism with particular emphasis on individualism and entrepreneurship. They focus on rewards for those who have worked hard, while arguing that the weaker members of society should generally fend for themselves. In the last 25 years, these two strains of beliefs have congealed in surprising ways to form the central moral foundation of the Republican Party.[2]

---

[2] Mahler, 2005; McKibben, 2005

In contrast, it is much more difficult to point to the religious or moral foundations of the Democratic Party. One of the most glaring errors on the part of the Party has been to largely ignore religious beliefs in reaching out to potential supporters. Even though a strong majority of Americans identify in some way with Judea-Christian religion, Progressive Christians are frequently discouraged from taking an active role in party politics and tying Progressive issues to Biblical tenets is rejected as nonintellectual. If Democrats were willing to make the Party more welcoming to those with religious convictions, strong alliances could be made with a large number of faith groups in the US, including mainline Protestant churches. As Rev. Jim Wallis points out in his book *God's Politics*, Democrats share fundamental concerns with these groups, like poverty, the environment, and social justice.

The clear convictions of Progressive Christians can help Democrats as they chart a stronger course and offer an authentic voice in the skirmishes over moral issues. In addition, Democratic candidates who talk openly and honestly about their faith reap political benefits. Democrat Tim Kaine's win in Virginia's 2005 gubernatorial race provides strong evidence of this. He bravely discussed the religious underpinnings of his anti-death penalty position, as well as articulated an anti-abortion stance, which focused on promoting adoption and economic support to low-income women. Bob Casey's faith has also been a consistent part of his platform in campaigning for a Senate seat in Pennsylvania.

Progressives who are not religious need to articulate strong moral convictions as well. These convictions could be most easily grounded in beliefs concerning *human nature*. Much of the populist rhetoric which effectively resonated with working class Americans in the 1930s was tied not only to religious beliefs, but also to moral beliefs. Such beliefs assumed that the average American was essentially good, while those in power tended towards corruption. The Populists' moral foundation allowed them to portray themselves as the party fighting for justice by

20

protecting the good and vulnerable worker from those who were powerful and corrupt. This remains a strong position from which to raise a convicted moral voice today.

Progressives need to use commonly held religious and moral beliefs to reclaim the values conversation in this country. There is mounting evidence that the American people are willing to listen to a new moral agenda. A Scripps poll conducted in February 2005 found that the top moral concerns for most Americans were child/spousal abuse and hunger. In addition, Americans were much more worried about greed than they were about homosexuality.

Values[3]

A person's beliefs are greatly influenced by their values – their fundamental judgments about right and wrong, good and bad. Values, to an even greater degree than beliefs, emanate from an individual's experience in society and can be very resistant to change. Some enduring American values identified by cultural theorists include:

Achievement and success
Americans value accomplishments and particularly honor those members of its society who achieve economic success.

Efficiency and practicality
Americans value work that is conducted in a reasoned and systematic way.

Progress
Americans value technical innovations and the notion of moving forward.

---

[3] Steele & Redding, 1962

Freedom
Americans value the right to set their own course in life, as well as freedom of association and freedom of speech.

Equality
Americans value equality of opportunity. Each person should have the opportunity to participate in the political process, education, and the pursuit of the American dream.

Individualism
Americans value the rights of the individual above the rights of society. Limitations on individual freedom should be kept at a minimum.

Effort and optimism
Americans value a positive attitude and hard work expended towards meeting goals.

A short review of American political discourse in the last 100 years will quickly yield countless examples of appeals to these cultural values.[4] For instance, one of the major characters in American political storytelling is the average American who despite all odds, struggles against adversity to eventually realize success. This one theme simultaneously embodies the values of *achievement and success, progress, freedom, effort and optimism, equality of opportunity, and individualism.* In crafting their persuasive appeals around these concepts, politicians have been able to signal that they share commonly held values with their audience.

Many of the contemporary examples of discourse which effectively incorporates these values have come from the Republican camp. Their success has been frustrating to most Progressives who note that Republican policies rarely reflect the values they espouse. For example, even though President Bush

---

[4] Our own decision to embrace *progressive* over *liberal* in the contemporary political sphere demonstrates the power of linking language with cultural values.

favors a constitutional amendment to ban gay marriage, he keyed on the American values of *individualism, freedom of choice,* and *equality* in the following response to a question concerning homosexuality in the 2004 debates:

"I do know that we have a choice to make in America and that is to treat people with tolerance and respect and dignity. It's important that we do that. I also know in our society, consenting adults can live the way they want to live. And that's to be honored." – George Bush, October 13th, 2005

This example aptly demonstrates the power of politically effective language. Such language gives Americans the impression that Republicans embrace particular values, even as their policies fly in the face of those very values.

Another example of the effective use of cultural values is found in the Republicans' decision to portray John Kerry as a pessimist early in the 2004 campaign. They understood that such a portrayal would be effective on two levels. First, because Americans generally value *optimism,* a candidate who is seen as pessimistic is also seen as an outsider to the culture. Second, Republicans knew that Kerry would have to respond to their accusations by defending himself as an optimist. In so doing, he reduced his ability to be overtly critical of the country's current condition. Any time Kerry would point out specific domestic or foreign policies that weren't working, the Republicans would respond by saying Kerry was negative and his pessimism was a liability the country could not afford. Even though he began on the offensive, the repeated labeling of him as a pessimist forced Kerry to play defense and essentially weakened his critique.

Bush responded to Kerry's criticism of the Iraq War using this approach in the 2004 debates. In the first debate Bush argued:

"You cannot expect to build an alliance when you denigrate the contributions of those who are serving side-by-side with American troops in Iraq."

He continued in this line of attack in the second debate:

"He talks about a grand idea: Let's have a summit; we're going to solve the problem in Iraq by holding a summit. And what is he going to say to those people that show up at the summit? Join me in the wrong war at the wrong time at the wrong place. Risk your troops for what you call a mistake. Nobody is going to follow somebody who doesn't believe we can succeed and somebody who says that the war we are in is a mistake."

Of course, Democrats appeal to many of the same values that Republicans do. The difference lies in what they apply those values to. In the last 25 years, Democrats have moved the issues that concern everyday Americans from the center of their policy and rhetorical agenda to the sidelines. They have replaced issues like the minimum wage, health care, and job security with issues like abortion, gay marriage, and the environment. As a result, Democrats end up talking about *equality* in terms of gay marriage rather than equal opportunity for the American Dream and *freedom* as the freedom to choose an abortion rather than freedom from the unfair treatment of workers by much of corporate America. Again, Progressives need to shift the agenda while keeping hold of the common values which resonate with the majority of Americans.

Behaviors[5]

Many of our behaviors can be traced to our cultural beliefs and values. In fact, how people act often reveals what they care most about. The following list marks some aspects of American culture that influence our behavior in our everyday lives. The list also

---

[5] Hammond and Morrison, 1996

demonstrates how our own everyday behaviors shape the expectations we bring to politics.

Demanding choices
Americans not only want to choose their representatives, they also relate choice to the way their tax dollars are spent and their children are educated.

Pursuing dreams
Americans want to be able to achieve economic success and dislike most government restrictions on business, and particularly small business.

Wanting more
Americans see the accumulation of wealth as a positive pursuit. They are also impressed by a technologically advanced military.

Displaying impatience with time
Americans want to see fast results from their political leaders. In addition, they expect simple messages they can easily digest.

Forgiving mistakes
Americans are often forgiving of their political figures. They give them the benefit of the doubt especially if they express regret or remorse.

Seeking innovation
Americans want innovative ideas from their political leaders. Voters look for creative solutions and bold new directions.

Politicians key on certain common behaviors when they tout themselves as "a new voice in government" or suggest that their opponent wants to limit various choices. They recognize that appealing to everyday behaviors and preferences not only builds common ground between them and their audience, but also allows persuaders to demonstrate that they will act in line with their constituents once they are elected.

The Bush Administration recognized these common American behaviors early on and effectively used them to advocate for certain policies. For example, many proponents of the Iraq War stressed the urgency of the situation, suggesting that there was little time for further negotiation. In September of 2002, Secretary of Defense Donald Rumsfeld displayed this urgency when he said "No terrorist state possesses a greater or more immediate threat to the security of our people and the stability of the world than the régime of Saddam Hussein in Iraq." Vice President Dick Cheney used similar appeals:

"Iraq is busy enhancing its capabilities in the field of chemical and biological agents, and they continue to pursue an aggressive nuclear weapons program. These are offensive weapons for the purpose of inflicting death on a massive scale, developed so that it Saddam Hussein can hold the threat over the head of anyone he chooses. What we must not do in the face of this mortal threat is to give it to wishful thinking or to willful blindness" – Dick Cheney, August 29th, 2002

In essence, Republicans appealed to the American behavior of *displaying impatience with time* to justify why immediate action was appropriate and other avenues should not be considered.

Another important example can be found in the Bush Administration's decision to send tax refund checks to almost all Americans. While these checks were, in reality, a drop in the bucket for many Americans struggling with debt, unemployment, and inflation, they did appeal to voters *demanding choices*, *pursuing dreams*, and *displaying impatience with time*. Bush capitalized on this in many of his persuasive appeals. For example, in the third debate in 2004 he reminded Americans:

"You've got more money in your pocket as a result of the tax relief we passed and he (Kerry) opposed. If you have a child, you got $1000 child credit. That's money in your pocket. It's your money…. And when you have more money in your pocket, you're able to better afford things you want. I believe the role of government is to stand side by side with our citizens to help them realize their dreams, not tell citizens how to live their lives." – George Bush, October 13th, 2004

Europe getting ahead of us

In the next election, Democrats should craft messages that largely appeal to Americans' tendency to *seek innovation*. Not only will we be in good position to point out what has not worked in terms of the old way of doing things (under Republican leadership across the board), we will have begun to re-craft our own party. As a result, we should be able to demonstrate to voters both how we differ from Republicans, and how we ourselves have changed. If we can focus on our own re-emergence, while at the same time contrasting our image with the legacy of the Republicans, we can truly offer an inviting new option. We must also use the next election to highlight our *commitment to choice*, consistently showing how our candidates will offer Americans a greater range of choices as they work to reinstate and expand civil liberties and personal freedoms.

Better Persuasion: 3 Things You Can Do

1) Develop a solid foundation from which to articulate strong/consistent moral beliefs.

Every Progressive must do the soul-searching necessary to craft political arguments based on moral beliefs. It is not enough to suggest that everyone is entitled to their opinion. Instead, if you are Progressive who is also a Christian, you need to align yourself with organizations like Sojourners (www.sojo.net), which is actively working to reclaim Christianity from the Right. As a Progressive Christian, you should bring your religious beliefs to the forefront of the political picture. If you are a Progressive who affiliates with another faith, you should join organizations like the Interfaith Alliance (www.interfaithalliance.org), which is building bridges between all types of faith communities, as well as calling them to be active in politics. Again, you should have your faith under gird the moral arguments you bring to the political realm. Finally, if you are Progressive who does not identify with a particular faith, you should still develop and articulate clear moral arguments, perhaps based on widely held beliefs concerning human nature. In the end, the key is to create a strong and clear foundation for your persuasive appeals and your policies.

2) Consistently highlight specific ways in which Republicans do not share key beliefs/values with the American people. Use their policy objectives as evidence for your claims.

For example:

- Americans value education, but Republicans are cutting school funding. How will we effectively compete in the global market without a strong education system (especially as many of our blue-collar jobs are going overseas)?
- Americans value hard work, but Republicans want to cut taxes like the estate tax which benefits the hyper-rich, many of whom have not worked for the money. How are we going to support small-business ventures when funds for such projects rely on the availability of some tax dollars?
- Americans value efficient and effective government, but Republicans have been rapidly expanding government bureaucracy and government spending without improving government services. Examples like the botched response to Hurricane Katrina reveal their approach is not getting the job done. How can Republicans honestly point the finger at Democrats for big and wasteful government?

3) Get together with other Progressives in your community and be prepared to respond to government service cuts at the state and local level. Demonstrate the impact of these cuts at the same time you showcase the Democrats' commitment to vulnerable populations and local communities.

Some examples of what you could do include:

- Set up a blanket drive when heating subsidies for the poor are cut. Wear T-shirts that read "Active Democrat Responding to More Republican Service Cuts" and hand out blankets and warm clothes.
- Clean up a local park when maintenance funding has been cut – pass out pamphlets explaining the cuts while you work.
- Take out a small ad in your local paper telling how the cuts have affected 1 or more vulnerable people in your neighborhood. Include a photo.

Explain that our program is voluntarily doing what govt should.

CHAPTER 2

HOW TO REASON WITH
AN UNREASONABLE VOTER

Argument is one of the oldest and most familiar tools used in political persuasion. Throughout history, many voices have maintained that the very foundation of democracy depends upon the electorate's ability to engage in logical reasoning and the candidates' willingness to argue for their positions. This perspective is widely held today, as most Americans expect candidates and those who speak on their behalf to present arguments and support those arguments with reasons and evidence. In addition, most Americans still believe that it is the side with the best arguments which will successfully persuade voters and win the election at the end of the day.

Surprisingly, argument has remained an important tool for political persuaders despite the fact that it is constantly diluted and distorted in the contemporary political sphere. Everyday we encounter literally thousands of persuasive messages, most of which we filter out. When we do evaluate a message, we are often forced to make decisions based on the persuader's half-stated claims, illogical reasoning, and incomplete evidence. As mass-mediated messages have filled our public spaces, this has become increasingly true. Mass-mediated appeals do not allow the receiver to ask for clarification, state objections, or demand additional evidence. In this context, we rarely find human beings making purely rational decisions or advancing arguments based solely on logical appeals.

As the amount of available information has increased dramatically, the difficulty of evaluating that information in a timely manner has also increased. Today, most Americans evaluate candidates and issues through 30-second ads. These ads often discourage reasoned decision making, relying instead on emotional language and dramatic graphics. Increasingly, these ads also make false claims or use blatantly misleading evidence without penalty from the Federal Communications Commission (FCC).[6]

Despite these conditions, a form of logical reasoning in political decision-making persists. Voters analyze and assess political issues using a variety of shortcuts in the reasoning process to cope with a high volume of complex and contradictory information. For their part, persuaders try to understand and influence this process. In the end, decision-making in the political sphere requires an uneven balance in which the persuader combines the components of argument with other approaches to persuasion, and the audience evaluates political messages based on a mix of logical reasoning and other factors including social networks, emotional impressions, and prior experience.[7]

Effective persuaders are able to recognize the fact that argument retains an important role in political persuasion, while at the same time accepting that such argument rests on a blend of rationality and emotional responses. Argument allows the persuader to move beyond presenting opinions to the building of a case. Persuaders utilize the key components of argument so they can increase their legitimacy, demonstrate support for their positions, and change an audience's mind by guiding them through the reasoning process. As such, argument makes a unique contribution to political persuasion.

Claims

The political process is full of people making claims. In any political contest, voters are typically trying to assess a candidate based on their previous record, their values, and their political

---

[6] Hall Jamieson, 2001
[7] Popkin, 1991

promises. These concerns are loosely tied to the three main types of claims available to a persuader: claims of fact, claims of value, and claims of policy.

Factual claims describe something that has existed in the world, currently exists, or is expected to exist in the future. Such claims can also be used to classify and define. For example, a persuader is making a factual claim when she points out: *The Bush Administration took America from a $236 billion surplus to a $375 billion deficit in 3 years.*[8]

Value claims are used to evaluate or judge something in the world. They can also compare the value of two things. A value claim concerning the deficit would sound more like: *Building such a high deficit is fiscally irresponsible.*

Policy claims suggest future actions that should be taken to deal with the current state of affairs. Such claims prescribe behavior and often use action-oriented verbs. An example of a policy claim on the topic would be: *We should cut the deficit in half over the next four years.*

Obviously, political persuasion requires the use of a variety of claims. Like every other persuasion technique, persuaders must assess the audience and context before deciding which type of claim to deploy. Political persuaders may use claims to answer questions, explain positions, or craft an image of themselves for the voters. In choosing claims, effective persuaders will recognize that some types of claims are easier to make than others.

Factual claims typically necessitate a large amount of evidence to support them. Whether the claim offers answers to controversial questions or speculates on a future state of affairs, the audience will expect a sufficient body of evidence in support

---

[8] budget.senate.gov/democratic/charts/2004/packet_deficitecon012004.pdf

of the argument. This can be a risky situation for the persuader if they do not have the time to present the evidence or the audience does not have enough interest to hear it.

In the same vein, policy claims come with their own costs. When the political persuader makes a policy claim, the audience can disregard that claim as an empty political promise, they can react negatively, feeling the proposed solution is flawed, or they can demand evidence as to how the persuader might fulfill that claim which incurs the same risks noted above. Policy claims also require greater accountability on the part of the persuader and they can be used against the persuader if they are not fulfilled.

In contrast, value claims do not require the persuader to provide the same level of evidence as factual claims, nor take the responsibility for future action required by policy claims. In addition, because value claims appear to reflect the moral positions of a persuader, they are often seen as more authentic. This is especially true when these claims are presented with strong conviction.

In looking at the last election it is easy to note that Democrats repeatedly relied on factual claims. They wanted to answer the electorate's questions by crafting factual arguments concerning the current economic state of the country, the invasion of Iraq, and the various misdeeds of the Bush Administration. They stated these facts time and time again and tried to provide evidence to back them up. It became evident rather quickly, however, that while most of these claims rested on credible and sufficient evidence, there was rarely the opportunity to present it. Even in the debates, where more time was available, such claims quickly became ineffective as one candidate would claim one thing and the other would claim the exact opposite. In the end, most voters did not have the time or the inclination to discover whose claim of fact was true and whose was not. They simply tuned out.

The Kerry campaign also tried to make a number of policy claims, both in *The Plan for America* and in shortened versions during speaking engagements. Many of the proposals, while innovative and potentially effective, were complex and difficult to explain. As a result, the average voter remained unconvinced that Kerry could enact these policies. In addition, the opposition responded to Kerry's policy claims by suggesting that they were empty promises that he either could not keep or would pursue at the expense of the American taxpayer. Because these claims reflect the pre-existing assumptions of many Americans (that candidates don't keep their word and Democrats raise taxes), they were accepted at face value with little or no evidence being required.

In contrast to the arguments put forth by the Democrats, Bush and other Republicans made a lot of value claims during the 2004 campaign. These types of claims were much safer to make and much easier to communicate. As value claims, they did not require substantial evidence, were difficult to challenge, and gave the American people the impression that they knew where the candidates stood on a variety of issues, even if they remained uncertain about the details. For example, during the third presidential debate both candidates were asked about the rising cost of health insurance. Notice the language Bush used in crafting his arguments:

"...there's a systemic problem. Health-care costs are on the rise because the consumers are not involved in the decision-making process. Most health-care costs are covered by third parties. And therefore, the actual user of health care is not the purchaser of health care. And there's no market forces involved with health care. It's one of the reasons I'm a strong believer in what they call health savings accounts. These are accounts that allow somebody to buy a low-premium, high-deductible catastrophic plan and couple it with tax-free savings. Businesses can contribute, employees can contribute on a contractual basis. But this is a way to make sure people are actually involved with the decision-making process on health care. Secondly, I do believe the lawsuits—I don't believe, I know—that the lawsuits are causing health-care costs to rise in America. That's why I'm such a strong believer in medical liability reform." -George Bush, October 13th, 2004

This response tells people very little about the current situation or the specific policies that will address it. What it does tell people about George Bush is that he values the freedom of people to make their own decisions, that he believes in the ability of market forces to properly allocate resources, and that he favors tax-free savings. It also tells voters that these values make him a *believer* in healthcare savings accounts and medical liability reform. His language is simple and his values, not his policies, are highlighted.

In general, Republicans are better at this type of language than Democrats. Compare the website statements regarding abortion by Democrat Ken Salazar with those of Pete Coors in the Senate race for Colorado:

"I do not support mandatory waiting periods, spousal consent, biased counseling requirements or other extreme limits on abortion rights. I do support parental notification, with appropriate bypass procedures, and bans on late term abortions, except when necessary to protect the life or health of the mother." -Ken Salazar

"I have a fundamental belief in the sanctity of human life. I am opposed to abortion" -Pete Coors

Progressives may tend to shy away from value claims because they feel that it is their policy positions that really matter at the end of the day. While this is certainly true, a good political persuader can advance value claims, which are more easily understood and accepted by the American public, at the same time he pursues a specific policy agenda. It is important to remember that talking in terms of values does not mean you must ignore good policy making.

Reasoning in Context

Arguments consist of reasons and are likewise built through a reasoning process that connects the claim and evidence. When someone advances a claim, reasons serve to answer the question *why*. As the previous example demonstrates, Pete Coors is opposed to abortion *because* he has a "fundamental belief in the sanctity of human life." Logical decision-making most often relies upon three types of reasoning: cause and effect (if you roll back environmental legislation, negative environmental consequences will follow), reasoning by sign (an increase in the intensity of natural disasters demonstrates the impact of global warming on the environment), and reasoning by analogy (if stronger environmental legislation in California reduced pollutants, such legislation will be effective in reducing pollutants in Florida). Because much of the reasoning process occurs automatically, people often come to decisions without fully knowing how they did so. This is particularly the case with public argument, which rarely follows a purely logical pattern, but instead accounts for the contingent, contextual nature of the sphere of human affairs. Under such conditions, the persuader often advances incomplete arguments, relying on the audience to fill in one or more parts from their own experience or from what is generally accepted within their society. For example, when a persuader argues that we should elect a candidate for federal office because they have strong foreign-policy experience, she assumes that the audience will fill in part of the argument, namely, that having foreign-policy experience is beneficial to someone holding federal office. Or, when someone argues that we should do more in this country to eliminate poverty, he does not have to make the case that poverty is a negative state of affairs. We already *know* that.

Given that much public argument rests upon what audience members take for granted, those assumptions become a key factor in the success or failure of many persuasive appeals. These assumptions, or commonly held knowledge do not spontaneously occur, but are deliberately created. If a persuader can control what is taken for granted in a society she reduces the difficulty of persuading her audience on any particular issue.

One of the most important things that Progressives can acknowledge at this point is how much ground we have lost in terms of influencing the central assumptions of our society. In line with arguments made by George Lakoff in *Don't Think of an Elephant! Know Your Values and Frame the Debate*, it is precisely this fundamental level of understanding and perspective that we have ignored for the last 25 years. As a result of our own silence and a persistent rhetorical strategy on the part of the Right, Republicans have been very successful in constructing our culture's common values and accepted knowledge over the past several decades. Some examples of these taken for granted notions include: the government wastes taxpayer dollars, liberals are elitist, corporate interest must be protected, a strong military acts as a deterrent, and our environment is a resource to be used. When an audience already accepts these premises, the work of the Republicans is made easier, while the work of the Progressives is made much more difficult.

When a persuader can assume that their audience is operating from shared common ground, they are at a great advantage. First, they are able to get their point across more quickly, which is key in a fast-paced, mediated world. Second, the speaker does not have to take responsibility for controversial positions. By allowing the audience to fill in the premises themselves, the speaker avoids being associated with potentially damaging statements. Third, persuaders who use this type of approach are often seen as more credible by the listeners because the views of the speaker are similar to those held by their audience. Finally, and most importantly, the audience is much more likely to be persuaded by arguments delivered in this manner because they have subconsciously contributed to the construction of the argument by providing the commonly accepted premise. In helping to build the argument, the audience becomes much more likely to buy it.

To recognize the power of this position, one only has to contrast the ease with which Bush convinced voters that Kerry would spend their money on expanding government programs to the difficulty that Kerry had in demonstrating, even with a lot of hard evidence, that Bush was spending exorbitant amounts of money and had created the biggest deficit the country had ever seen. When asked during the third debate in 2004 how the candidates would confront the deficit, Kerry was forced to offer a long and complex explanation:

"I'll tell you exactly how I can do it: by reinstating what President Bush took away, which is called pay as you go. During the 1990s, we had pay-as-you-go rules. If you were going to pass something in the Congress, you had to show where you are going to pay for it and how.... Every plan that I have laid out—my health-care plan, my plan for education, my plan for kids to be able to get better college loans—I've shown exactly how I'm going to pay for those.... We shut the loophole which has American workers actually subsidizing the loss of their own job. They just passed an expansion of that loophole in the last few days: $43 billion of giveaways, including favors to the oil and gas industry and the people importing ceiling fans from China. I'm going to stand up and fight for the American worker. And I am going to do it in a way that's fiscally sound. I show how I pay for the health care, how we pay for the education." -John Kerry, October 13th, 2004

Bush, on the other hand, was able to appeal to the widely held assumption that liberals tax and spend and then offer a simple claim regarding his own deficit reduction plan:

"Well, his rhetoric doesn't match his record. He talks about PAYGO. I'll tell you what PAYGO means, when you're a senator from Massachusetts, when you're a colleague of Ted Kennedy, pay go means: You pay, and he goes ahead and spends. He's proposed $2.2 trillion of new spending, and yet the so-called tax on the rich, which is also a tax on many small-business owners in America, raises $600 million by our account—billion, $800 billion by his account. There is a tax gap. And guess who usually ends up filling the tax gap? The middle class.... I proposed a detailed budget, Bob. I sent up my budget man to the Congress, and he says, here's how we're going to reduce the deficit in half by five years. It requires pro-growth policies that grow our economy and fiscal sanity in the halls of Congress." – George Bush, October 13th, 2004

The key to successfully utilizing this type of reasoning is to understand and influence what serves as common knowledge or shared cultural values. Despite the rhetorical push on the part of the Republicans, remnants of liberal notions and values remain. Examples of these include a commitment to equality and an inclination towards compassion. Because we need to undo much of the work of our opponents, we need to consistently return to these concepts in clear and obvious ways until such notions replace more conservative ones. While it takes time and a lot of persuasive effort to change a society's common sense, the rewards are great. As we will see in the chapter on framing, Progressives should view this as a complex and long-term approach to reclaiming the hearts and minds of Americans.

Evidence–Fudged Numbers and True Stories

Perhaps the most important and most obvious part of building an argument is the presentation of evidence. Claims that are not supported by evidence are essentially relegated to matters of opinion. As a result, those employing logical appeals must marshal an array of evidence pieces they can use to advance their argument at any given time. Thankfully, persuaders have a variety to choose from. Just as there are several types of claims, there are also several types of evidence that can be applied to an argument. In addition to using an audience's pre-existing beliefs, common knowledge, and direct experience, the persuader can also employ facts, statistics, testimony (expert/eyewitness), examples, and specific instances/stories. These different types of evidence allow for a speaker to support the claim from a variety of angles. For example, many Progressive voices have made the policy claim that we should bring our troops home from Iraq and use the death of American soldiers as their primary reason. Such advocates can support this claim with different types of evidence:

Facts: Many members of the military are serving longer terms than expected because of the Bush Administrations Stop-gap policy.

Statistics: There were 84 military fatalities in Iraq in November, 2005.

Testimony: "The war in Iraq is not going as advertised. It is a flawed policy wrapped in illusion. The American public is way ahead of us. The United States and coalition troops have done all they can in Iraq, but it is time for a change in direction. Our military is suffering. The future of our country is at risk. We cannot continue on the present course. It is evident that continued military action in Iraq is not in the best interest of the United States of America, the Iraqi people or the Persian Gulf Region." -John Murtha, November 17th, 2005

Examples: Staff Sergeant Rene Ledesma, aged 34, was killed on May 15, 2004 by hostile fire in Baghdad.

Specific instances: "This morning I visited with the family of Darius Jennings, a courageous young man who gave his life this week in Iraq. He is the third graduate of Orangeburg-Wilkinson High School to give his life for our country in Iraq. It's clear that Darius was a caring man, who loved his family and his country. We are all grateful for his service and we should honor it today." -Wesley Clark, November 6th, 2003

While audience and context will typically impact a persuader's choice of evidence, most arguments rely on a mixture of evidence types. It is important to note that like claims, some types of evidence are easier to use and typically more effective than others. One of the most important trends for political persuaders to be aware of is the diminished authority of facts and statistics in the eyes of the American public. In the contemporary political picture, most voters are rather suspicious of these types of evidence, in part because they recognize the inherent complexity of such data. Realizing that in order to fully assess the credibility of the facts and statistics put before them they would have to know much more about the data than the persuader tells them, the average American quickly dismisses such evidence. In addition, voters are aware that such factors as question formulation, study funders, and partial reporting impact this type of data. Because the public is continually confronted with conflicting numbers or disputed facts, they generally tune out rather than trying to discern who is telling the truth.

Today, the logical power of facts and statistics has been replaced by the emotional power of examples and stories. There are many reasons for this shift. Part of the explanation lies in the prevalence and familiarity of emotion in other persuasive appeals, particularly those made by advertisers and the news media. As the American public has been exposed to more examples and stories and fewer facts and statistics, they have come to expect those types of data in support of all arguments made in the public sphere. In addition, research suggests that emotional responses can be processed much faster than logical ones. In our fast-paced and message cluttered lives, the data which is processed most quickly will often be the data which is most effective. Finally, similar to value claims, persuaders can use this type of evidence to their advantage as it is much more difficult to dispute. In fact, it is frequently regarded as the most authentic type of evidence, particularly when an audience can relate to it based on their own personal experience.

In the last election, Democrats assumed that the American public would be outraged when they heard the facts and figures. Just as they decided to use factual and policy claims, they also relied heavily upon factual and statistical evidence. Progressive persuaders often deployed statistical evidence even as they acknowledged how unreliable such evidence could be.[9] Republicans, on the other hand, often used examples and stories. For instance, in a televised debate between Betty Castor and Mel Martinez for the Florida Senate seat, Mel Martinez responded to a question about importing drugs from Canada by saying:

"...if our seniors–let me tell you, I have three moms: my natural mother and two foster mothers. They are all now in their seventies and eighties. These are strong women that I love and respect. And anything I can do for them so they can get the prescription drugs they need as cheaply as they can, I will do it."
-Mel Martinez, October 18th, 2004

Progressives need to capitalize on the power of stories. We need to use stories not simply to tug on the audience's heartstrings, but also to better reveal who we are and what we stand for. We need to let personal narratives, our own and others, support our arguments whenever possible. Barack Obama does an excellent job of this in his Senate debate with Alan Keyes. He responds to a direct question regarding the controversial topic of sex education by relaying his own experience:

"We have an existing law that mandates sex education in the schools. We want to make sure that it's medically accurate and age-appropriate. Now, I'll give you an example, because I have a six-year-old daughter and a three-year-old daughter, and one of the things my wife and I talked to our daughters about is the possibility of somebody touching them inappropriately, and what that might mean... And that was included specifically in the law, so that kindergartners are able to exercise some possible protection against abuse, because I have family members as well

---

[9] John Kerry, in the third debate, said in rebuttal to Bush's claim that he had increased taxes 98 times and busted the budget 277 times: "anybody can play with these votes. Everybody knows that."

as friends who suffered abuse at that age. So, that's the kind of stuff that I was talking about in that piece of legislation."
-Barack Obama, October 21st, 2004

Another example can be found in Senator Salazar's decision to incorporate a constituent's story in comments he made regarding Social Security:

"Recently, President Bush and Republicans in Congress traveled across the country to sell the public on his plan to privatize Social Security. But the plan he is offering won't even come close to putting the program on solid financial footing. In fact, his plan for privatization would lead to a 40 percent cut in current benefits for middle-class beneficiaries, add five trillion dollars to our national debt, and make the system weaker in the future…. As we debate this issue in Congress, I will always take the words of Amelia Valdez from Pueblo to heart. She gave me a photograph of President Roosevelt signing the Social Security Act into law in 1935 and with tears in her eyes she said to me: 'Hang it in your office as a reminder—please, do not let them dismantle my only source of income.' I promised her I wouldn't, and I and my Democratic colleagues intend to keep that promise. It will take hard work, but it can be done. -John Salazar, August 13th, 2005

By using more examples and specific stories, we will create messages that not only resonate with our audience, but also remain with them, influencing their attitudes and behaviors as they go to the polls.

Pointing the Political Finger

In political argument, there are several ways to confront the opposition directly. One approach is to make claims about your opponent's record which can be done by highlighting poor policy decisions, negative consequences, or a marked difference between what was promised and what was actually delivered. Another approach is to refute the arguments offered by your opponent through the use of opposing evidence which disproves their original argument.

In a political campaign, it is only natural that part of the persuader's energy will be spent on making claims regarding his opposition or refuting his opponent's points and positions. The problem arises when the persuader chooses to spend the majority of his time in this way. In the 2004 election, Democrats relied heavily on these practices, often choosing to point out the problems of their opponents rather than offering their own claims. This was particularly true in the presidential campaign. Persuaders, from the candidate himself to those knocking on doors or hosting house parties, focused on the problems of the Bush Administration and their misleading statements. In Kerry's own stump speeches, he would often introduce his agenda only briefly before turning to a long list of the problems facing America under the Bush Administration. In addition, many of the people campaigning for Kerry knew very little about his policies, depending instead on a mindset that became known as *Anybody But Bush*.

We must make sure we do not make the same mistake again. Building a campaign primarily in opposition to the other candidate is insufficient and ineffective. It also creates a strong sense of negativity that rarely inspires people. One of the most important things Progressive persuaders can do prior to any election is to craft strong but simple arguments. These arguments should be based on their own claims, rather than depend upon oppositional argument. Successful campaigns cannot be built on the failures of other candidates. The current political context requires candidates who can present themselves to the public as strong leaders with innovative ideas, reasoned principles that resonate with the American public and persuasive evidence that make sense to the voters. Progressives must start now to do the long-term work of building arguments that both persuade and energize voters.

Better Persuasion: 3 Things You Can Do

1) Craft 3 value claims and support them with reasons based on common knowledge and shared values.

Progressives must be more courageous about making value claims. We need to speak from the heart and persuade others based on our convictions. The best place to start is with a review of your own set of values. After writing down several values, choose 3 that can be supported by reasons taken from our shared cultural values and knowledge.

For example:

- I believe Social Security is a valuable program BECAUSE it enables seniors to maintain some independence and rewards them for the hard work of their earlier years.
- I believe in public education BECAUSE it creates a foundational point for equal opportunity and allows each child to try and reach her potential.
- I believe that the church is an important American institution but one that needs to be separate from the state BECAUSE everyone must have the right to choose their own spiritual path based on their own conscience.

2) Formulate 3 questions to disrupt assumptions that hurt the Progressive agenda.

Questions can be a powerful tool especially when they demonstrate your own commitments while at the same time putting the opposition on the defensive. In fact, many of the interpretations of our common ground exist only because they have never been challenged. This is clearly demonstrated by the power of questions regarding the Iraq War. The more Progressives ask, "What is victory?" the more upset the Republicans become and the more aware the public becomes that a clear answer to that question is vital. Every Progressive can begin to loosen the power of the Republicans' rhetorical position by crafting question and consistently asking them in public.

For example:

- How can we support our troops if we cannot buy the military equipment they need because corporations and wealthy Americans don't want to pay their fair share of taxes?
- Why do conservative Christians care more about the private lives of homosexual than they do about poverty?
- Do we really want to scale back our government to the point where we are unable to respond to disasters such as Hurricane Katrina or a potential pandemic like the bird flu?

3) For every claim you make find an appealing true story to tell your audience.

For example, in support of value claims concerning the importance of universal health-care, you could tell the story of one American's experience:

"Mary Wood of Depoe Bay was uninsured for many years. Mary had precancerous cells found twice and a family history of cancer, but without health insurance she could not afford to see a doctor for preventative screenings. Mary made too much to qualify for free screenings and too little to afford a $300 or 400 test. She went nine years without a mammogram or annual exam, but not without fear. As Mary explains living without out insurance she was in constant fear, 'the fear of something major happening and not being able to deal with it.' Mary also has a thyroid problem that requires medication. Without health insurance she didn't go to the doctor and went without her prescription for three years. 'Without insurance, I couldn't afford to go to the doctor, let alone afford the prescription if I went,' says Mary. Last April, Mary gained insurance through her employer. She has had a mammogram, an annual exam and even went to the doctor last winter when she got the flu. It has helped ease her fears."

-Oregonians for Health Security, June 9th, 2005

CHAPTER 3

THE POWER OF OUR NATIONAL NARRATIVE

Stories make for powerful persuasion. The prominence of anecdote in our public debate and private convictions suggests that humans often rely on stories rather than rational arguments. Every culture uses stories as part of their communication system and people often rely on these stories to understand and relay their experience. The narrative form is based on a structure with a beginning, middle, and end, as well as narrative elements such as characters, plots, themes, and narrators. It is primarily through the exchange of narratives that every member works to create and reinforce the substance of their culture.

In a society based on the sharing of narratives, people must constantly assess the stories they are told. Generally, the more important the story is to an audience, the more likely they will try to evaluate it, measuring the story's coherence and fidelity.[10] According to Walter Fisher (1984), people can judge *coherence* by asking themselves whether the story seems to make sense within itself. They look for overall consistency, as well as

---

[10] An example of how poor rhetoric can undermine the fidelity of a narrative and the credibility of its authors can be found in the exaggeration and overstatement used by Democrats during the last presidential campaign. Many Democrats argued that a second term for the Bush Administration would mean a return to the draft, the overturning of Roe v. Wade, and the rollback of the Endangered Species Act. While making a strong case for a crisis or calamity may seem like a good way to motivate voters at the time, it often backfires in the long run. This is because many of these things will probably not actually happen before the next election. As reality clearly contradicts the original narrative, that narrative loses its fidelity and the persuader loses their credibility. As a result, many voters may not feel compelled to vote in future elections or believe the arguments presented.

reliable and predictable characters. Likewise, Fisher suggests that people can measure the *fidelity* of a story based on whether the story is believable given their own experience. An audience evaluates the fidelity of various narratives so they can form attitudes and take specific actions. When confronted with two very different narratives concerning the same topic, the audience must decide which of the stories makes more sense to them.

Persuaders are well aware that stories often compete with one another to gain an audience's acceptance. This is particularly true for political persuasion where parties and candidates use narratives to present specific versions of the world we live in. These persuaders not only craft different stories concerning various issues, they also offer very different overarching narratives. Once again, common ground plays a key role. The persuader who has been able to shape the audience's commonly held beliefs will be much more effective in having her narrative accepted. As Andrew Fletcher, the Scottish patriot, said: "If one person was able to write the ballads (stories) of the country, he would not need to care who makes the laws." While commonly accepted narratives can be difficult to challenge, they can be changed or replaced by persistent persuaders over time.

Many of the stories circulating throughout American culture are derived from or depend upon our national narrative for their resonance. This national narrative offers a broad and enduring story that political persuaders often use to bind citizens together in a common identity, as well as direct their actions towards common purposes. The national narrative is largely taken for granted, with the values that underpin it seamlessly serving as guides for the audience to evaluate other stories. While every narrative is comprised of several elements that essentially make it a story, the key features of our national narrative are *setting*, *plot*, and *characters*.

Setting—Mythic America

A narrative's setting offers audience members a sense of where and when the story unfolds. Playing a prominent role in the story, it often affects other narrative aspects including the story's characters, mood, and tone. In the case of our national narrative, the setting of America's story represents how Americans understand their country, its past, its present, and its potential future. It also represents what we, as Americans, value. As such, setting is tied to myth which weaves together a society's life, history, and culture. Myth in this sense does not refer to that which is untrue, but rather to the narrative which tells the story of a whole culture. As myth defines our place and what it means to be part of that place, it shapes an audience's perception of their culture's unique setting. Roderick Hart (1990) identifies 4 primary types of myths which help create a sense of identity and place for the audience: *cosmological myths* (stories about our origin), *societal myths* (stories that illustrate right conduct), *identity myths* (stories about the uniqueness of a culture), and *eschatological myths* (stories about the future).

Perhaps the most important aspect of American mythology is the belief that America is a chosen nation. This belief emerges from our *cosmological and eschatological myths* rooted in Christianity, our *societal myths* regarding good and evil, and most clearly our *identity myths* concerning our unique role in the world. Radical conservatives like Jerry Falwell often aggressively advance this belief. Following the September 11th attacks, Falwell famously referred to "a veil of protection that God had placed around the nation as reward for its good deeds throughout history" and then suggested the veil had been lifted because of the activities of feminists and pagans. While few political persuaders would make the controversial claims Falwell does, Republicans routinely appeal to the chosen nation concept. For example, Ronald Reagan popularized the image of America standing alone in the world as "the shining city on a hill." In his farewell speech to the nation, Reagan explained what he meant by the term:

"I've spoken of the shining city all my political life, but I don't know if I ever quite communicated what I saw when I said it. But in my mind it was a tall proud city built on rocks stronger than oceans, wind-swept, God-blessed, and teeming with people of all kinds living in harmony and peace, a city with free ports that hummed with commerce and creativity, and if there had to be city walls, the walls had doors and the doors were open to anyone with the will and the heart to get here." -Ronald Reagan, January 11th, 1989

Following September 11th, George W. Bush went beyond Reagan's suggestion that God favors America, to argue that America has been called to serve a unique purpose:

"And many have discovered again that even in tragedy—especially in tragedy—God is near. In a single instant, we realized that this will be a decisive decade in the history of liberty, that we've been called to a unique role in human events. Rarely has the world faced a choice more clear or consequential. Steadfast in our purpose, we now press on. We have known freedom's price. We have shown freedom's power. And in this great conflict, my fellow Americans, we will see freedom's victory." -George Bush, January 29th, 2002

Democrats, on the other hand, have generally shied away from the myth of America as a chosen nation. There are several reasons for this including the fact that many Progressives don't believe in the Christian basis of the mythology and others find the concept too arrogant or too often used to justify aggressive foreign policy initiatives. Unfortunately, we have forfeited the power of this myth solely because we disagree with how it is being deployed by our opposition. This has come at a cost. There is no doubt that good story telling in American politics reflects and reinforces the myths that characterize America as a place. These myths are both familiar to Americans and important in crafting their own identity. In addition, they offer Americans a sense of unity and stability because myths echo the language that binds our society together. In order to tell better stories which effectively resonate with the average American, Progressives must be willing to explore and accept many of the central myths which characterize the setting of our national narrative—the place that is America. The key is to re-craft what makes America a chosen nation, focusing on the broad aspect of strong leadership rather than the narrow one of military might.

Plot—Persistence of the American Dream

Perhaps the most essential aspect of any story is its plot, the unique sequence of events which unfolds as the storyline progresses. It is the plot that makes the story dynamic and keeps the reader's interest piqued; however, even as the plot changes, some aspects of the storyline remain constant. This is particularly true of national narratives in which characters and activities are continually changing, but values and goals remain the same. Political persuaders use the plot of our national narrative to their advantage, often encouraging certain behaviors. They intentionally craft a national story in which the characters are involved in similar courses of action that lend stability to the society at large.

One aspect of our national narrative that continues to endure is the American Dream. The American Dream provides a central element of our national plot, telling Americans what they should be striving for, and what the country values as a whole. This plot line contends that regardless of the conditions into which a person is born, if she works hard enough she will be able to achieve success. This success is evidenced by home ownership, marriage and family, and economic self-sufficiency. Americans typically accept this plot and reinforce it in their own behavior and their judgment of others. As a result, Americans who do not achieve these goals are generally looked down upon and blamed for their own failure. As our national plot, the American Dream assumes many things such as equality of opportunity, rational choice making, and the ability of the individual to overcome the most adverse of circumstances. Even when it is clear that these conditions do not exist, the American Dream is so powerful that people will strive to fulfill it by borrowing money they cannot repay and working for decades in jobs they do not like. In addition, Americans believe in the value of the American Dream to such a degree that they often assume that other countries would pursue the same plot line if given the opportunity.

And yet, not only are we encountering problems as we try to export this plot, the American Dream is also growing more and more elusive to the average American. In 2000 the Census Bureau reported that 31.5% of families in this country have a total income below $35,000 with the average per capita income being $21,857. Such income levels demonstrate that home ownership and other signs of economic self-sufficiency are impossible for most people in contemporary America. In addition, analysts note a growing gap between the wealthy and the poor. A recent study by the Institute for Policy Studies shows that executive pay rose by 571% between 1991 and 2000 while workers pay during that same period by only 37%.

Even as the reality of these numbers grows starker, political persuaders and other voices in our society keep the plot line of the American Dream alive. Success stories of people like Oprah Winfrey or Sam Walton who went from poverty to immense wealth, reinforce the potential of achieving the American Dream, if only everybody would work just a little bit harder. But the Dream also endures because the average American is not willing to give up the hope that is embedded within it. In a 1999 Newsweek poll, 41% of surveyed Americans thought that it was somewhat or very likely they would become wealthy. In essence, every American wants to believe that the American Dream will come true.

Political persuaders recognize the persistent power of the American Dream and capitalize upon it whenever possible. They encourage American citizens to take part in the plot, as well as identify themselves as the party/candidate who is most likely to enable Americans to achieve the Dream. While all Americans are familiar with the Dream, effective persuaders recognize that some audiences are more influenced by its power than others. Immigrant audiences, many of whom came to this country because of this aspect of our national narrative, are especially open to this appeal. In addition, candidates who themselves are immigrants often relate their own stories of the American Dream. Arnold Schwarzenegger offers an example of this in his 2004 speech at the Republican National Convention:

"My fellow Americans, this is an amazing moment for me. To think that a once scrawny boy from Austria could grow up to become governor of California and stand in Madison Square Garden to speak on behalf of the President of the United States. That is an immigrant's dream. It is the American Dream."
-Arnold Schwarzenegger, August 31st, 2004

Similar to our response regarding America as a chosen nation, Democrats have also had trouble talking about the American Dream in recent years. This is essentially because many of us recognize how quickly that dream is fading away. We feel uncomfortable in perpetuating a storyline we no longer believe in. So we evoke it, but hint at its demise:

"One month from today, the American dream is on the ballot.... Not too long ago this dream was within reach of all those willing to work for it. But today, for too many families, the dream is harder to reach because of decisions made by this Administration. -John Kerry, October 2nd, 2004

"I stand here tonight ready to work with you and John to make America strong again. And we have so much work to do. Because the truth is, we still live in two different Americas: one for people who have lived the American Dream and don't have to worry, and another for most Americans who work hard and still struggle to make ends meet." -John Edwards, July 28th, 2004

And yet, the American Dream will persist as part of our plot line. We must find a productive balance between keeping the hope of that dream alive and activating voters in the face of its disappearance. One effective approach (which will be further explored in the coming pages) would be for Progressive to craft a populist rhetoric that would optimistically frame the opportunity of the American Dream, at the same time inciting indignation that the greed of a few has reduced the potential for many to achieve that dream. Oregon Congressman Peter DeFazio does this quite well when he says:

"The President needs to quit promoting top-down class warfare. His plan would give a tax cut equivalent of a Yukon Denali XL with heated leather seats to the top one percent, and an oil lube and tune-up for the old jalopy to the average citizen." – Peter DeFazio, February 8th, 2001

Characters—Heroes, Villains, and Victims

Successful storytelling has always depended in part on the storyteller's ability to make her characters come to life for the audience. Audiences are looking for characters they can relate to, characters they can understand and pass judgment on. In this vein, stories are often comprised of a simplified cast of characters, which includes heroes, villains, and victims. Throughout history and across cultures, the creation of such characters has been very effective in political persuasion. Those holding political power have used these basic characterizations to secure support, justify suspect policies, and squelch dissent. Our own national narrative is no exception. National crises or conflicts are explained to the American people in terms of a struggle between the American hero (and sometimes victim) and enemies, which are cast as evil villains. Jewett and Lawrence (2003) lay out six sets of enduring expectations regarding heroes and villains, which are found in our national narrative, as well as the narratives of other cultures:

1) Heroes are on the good side, while villains are on the bad in an enduring struggle.
2) Heroes act to defend victims, while villains take the offensive.
3) Heroes are clean (in appearance and fighting techniques), while villains are dirty.
4) Heroes abide by the law, while villains act lawlessly.

55

5) Heroes are faithful to ideals and principals, while villains disregard them.
6) Heroes are humble, while villains are arrogant.

Similar to the construction of heroes and villains, victims also display certain characteristics. Victims are typically "good people" who are vulnerable to attack or at the mercy of conditions they cannot control. As such, victims are often portrayed as having done nothing to provoke the villain; they were just in the wrong place at the wrong time. This characterization of the victim allows the audience to easily identify with them, encouraging the listener to say, "That could be me."

In crafting central characters for the American narrative, there are many unwritten guidelines that persuaders should observe. First, it is important that political persuaders never overtly cast themselves as the hero. It just doesn't work. Instead, the persuader constructs a story where the country is a heroine or ordinary citizens act in extraordinary ways. The persuader should also reference heroes who are protecting their fellow citizens, such as police, and firefighters, and military servicemen.

In addition, the persuader must portray the average American as being both a potential hero and a potential victim. This encourages his audience to feel two very powerful emotions –pride and fear. In addition, it casts all potentially aggressive acts as self-defense. Much of the storytelling around the Iraq War not only keyed on heroes, military and otherwise, but also created potential victims by encouraging fear regarding future attacks. For example:

"We have seen the depth of our enemies' hatred in videos, where they laugh about the loss of innocent life. And the depth of their hatred is equaled by the madness of the destruction they design. We have found diagrams of American nuclear power plants and public water facilities, detailed instructions for making chemical weapons, surveillance maps of American cities, and thorough

descriptions of landmarks in America and throughout the world."
-George Bush, January 29th, 2002

Finally, the political persuader must also turn the enemy
into a clear villain. In characterizing these villains, political
persuaders generally take pains to highlight how the villains differ
from the average American often by dehumanizing them with
such labels as *barbarians* or *animals*. They also associate the enemy
with brutal acts like rape and murder. Douglas Kellner chronicles
this in his book *The Persian Gulf TV War* (1992). Specifically, he
demonstrates how the fabricated story of Iraqi soldiers taking
babies from incubators at a Kuwaiti hospital effectively
galvanized support for the first Gulf War. The American public
reacted strongly to these evil acts and readily supported military
actions against who they perceived to be such heartless villains.

The main narrative of the 2004 election involved our
response to September 11th and our role in the Middle East.
Because Republicans were in power during the September 11th
attack, they were in a position to craft the characters of that story.
The attack provided the perfect opportunity for the Republicans
to tell a simplified story to the American people, which placed
America in the role of hero, Muslim extremists in the role of
villain, and innocent American citizens as victims and potential
victims. During the election, the American people heard the same
story, with the same character construction over and over:
America, as a chosen nation and with President Bush at the helm,
will save the country and the world from the evil enemies of
terror by spreading freedom. Because the story was so clearly in
line with our existing myths, the Republicans easily transferred
these characterizations to the Iraq War despite the clear lack of
evidence connecting the two.

In addition to constructing a simple narrative, which
made sense to many Americans (largely because it fit into their
pre-existing notions regarding the Middle East), the Republicans
also made good rhetorical choices regarding some of the details
of that narrative. Most importantly, they constructed a campaign
discourse that focused primarily on external villains. Their villains

were always non-specified terrorists, Saddam Hussein, Al-Quaida, Osama Bin Laden, even France. They consistently chose to vilify these enemies rather than focus their attention on potential internal enemies. This was a clever move, which recognized the power of the current context—a nation at war, which was bitterly divided but wanted desperately to be united. They also recognized that although our alliances were central to our foreign policy in the past, September 11th changed that in the minds of many Americans. Because we alone were attacked on that day, we felt we alone could respond. We needed to settle the score on our own, lest we be seen in the role of victim and lose status on the world stage. George Bush's remarks during the first debate succinctly embody the Republicans' consistent narrative:

"This nation of ours has got a solemn duty to defeat this ideology of hate. And that's what they are. This is a group of killers who will not only kill here, but kill children in Russia, that'll attack unmercifully in Iraq, hoping to shake our will. We have a duty to defeat this enemy. We have a duty to protect our children and grandchildren. The best way to defeat them is to never waver, to be strong, to use every asset at our disposal, is to constantly stay on the offensive, and at the same time, spread liberty." -George Bush, September 30th, 2004

Because September 11th did not happen on the Democrats' watch, we were much less able to influence how the story was told. We struggled in trying to take ownership of the story, both because it seemed like we were playing catch-up and because many of us never accepted the simplified version in the first place. While we couldn't claim the story for ourselves, we also struggled in trying to challenge it. Whenever Democrats pointed out exaggerations like our success in winning the hearts and minds of Iraqis, scandals like those at the Abu Ghraib prison, or the fact that the US ignored the UN when it declared Iraq War, we were met with opposition and resistance regardless of the evidence presented.

In addition to the difficulties we had regarding the overarching narrative, Democrats made some bad choices in characterization at other levels. Most obviously, the decision to cast President Bush as an enemy fell flat in a time of uncertainty. Many Americans were looking for leadership and were therefore reluctant to accept that their President was another enemy they had to be wary of. In the same vein, the decision to focus on international bodies as offering more protection, essentially casting them as the hero, did not sit well with a country whose pride had already been bruised.

Better Persuasion: 3 Things You Can Do

1) Learn to be a better storyteller, especially in terms of the national narrative.

It is clear that many Americans best understand their country and its political leaders in terms of an overarching national narrative. With this in mind, every Progressive needs to incorporate narrative elements into their persuasion. These elements should recognize the enduring aspects of America story, particularly in terms of setting, plot, and character. Some simple suggestions for crafting effective narratives include:

- The simpler the story, the better
- The more often repeated, the more believable
- The more the audience can identify with the main character, the more they will like the story
- The more clearly it is tied to aspects of the national narrative, the faster it will be recognized and accepted

2) Find 3 ways to tell America's story in language that reflects Progressive ideals.

While it is never easy to re-craft key elements of a national narrative, certain contexts offer greater opportunities. The last several years have been very challenging for America and the average American: the Iraq War–its casualties and costs, scandals in corporate America, the explosion of the deficit, Hurricane Katrina, and rising levels of underemployment and poverty. While it has been difficult for Americans to accept that these factors are changing America's story, the opportunity for an honest assessment of the past and a new approach to the future is emerging. Progressives should be at the forefront in re-crafting essential elements of America's story. Here are some preliminary ways in which this might be done:

- Offer a setting for America in which it is a chosen nation based not on its military power, but on its courageous leadership. Part of the way in which that leadership is demonstrated is by taking responsibility for previous choices and charting a new course. In re-crafting America's setting, Progressives must remember what they love about America and refuse to cast it in a wholly negative light.

- Recognize the persistent plot line of the American Dream. Talk about the conditions necessary to realize the dream like equal opportunity, as well as government priorities that foster the dream. In order for the American Dream to stay alive, we must talk openly and honestly about difficult topics like greed and the influence of corporations on American life. Until we create the space for such discussions, the Dream will continue to fade away.

- Create a different heroic America. In public discourse America will always have to be the hero. Instead of casting America as the villain, we need to focus on what characteristics make for a heroic country and craft a country Americans can be proud of.

3) Find an everyday working class hero and tell their story over and over again.

Re-craft American heroism and cast it in terms of the average American. In a populist vein this is an important rhetorical move. Rather than consistently casting the working class in the role of victim, Progressives should portray them as heroes. For example, construct a story in which a working mother is the hero – noting how she manages to work each day, all the while offering security and direction to her children. Such a woman is an everyday American hero. All of us know someone like her. Let's tell her story.

CHAPTER 4

THE FRAMING OF POLITICS

If there is one tool of political persuasion you are already familiar with, it is probably framing. Following the election, George Lakoff's book, *Don't Think of an Elephant! Know Your Values and Frame the Debate*, captured the attention of Democrats eager to understand why their persuasive appeals failed to elect Progressive candidates across the board. Lakoff argues that the brain processes information through the use of frames: "One of the fundamental findings of cognitive sciences is that people think in terms of frames and metaphors–conceptual structures like those we have been describing. The frames are the synapses of our brains–physically present in the form of neural circuitry." - George Lakoff, March 18th, 2003. These frames are activated by certain language choices.

Even though most persuaders might find it difficult to understand the science behind frames, many are well aware of how effective they can be. Persuaders intentionally frame their messages to key on the parts of a story they want told and consistently highlight those parts for the audience they are trying to persuade. These dual activities, selecting and highlighting, allow the persuader to narrow the frame of debate in a variety of ways from defining what the problem is, to assigning responsibility for the problem to specific people, to promoting certain solutions.

Good persuaders take framing seriously. They construct their messages, both verbally and visually, to guide their audience's perceptions. As Lakoff suggests in his book, language can influence framing at a foundational level of values or at a simpler level of specific policies. Framing is very effective in contemporary persuasion because people will often rely on the frames created by others when they have no direct experience with the topic or the issue is very complex.

Political persuaders can be particularly successful in framing because Americans feel they should have opinions on issues affecting the country, but in truth very rarely have first-hand experience with most of the topics under debate. Of course, in reality, almost all political issues are quite broad and complex, but effective political persuaders are always working to narrow and simplify the issue. As a persuader consistently presents an issue in one way, the audience comes to interpret information through that frame, rejecting those facts that do not fit the frame. This is why framing is so powerful—if you can impact an audience's overarching frame on a topic you have much less work to do in any given persuasive attempt.

Unfortunately for Democrats, there is a lot of evidence that Conservatives have been more successful than Progressives at framing in recent decades. Conservatives have been able to say what problems Americans should be concerned with (set the agenda), point the finger at who is to blame, and direct our attention to a limited number of solutions. Take for example a 2005 cover story by U.S. News & World Report on religion and politics. The story listed the hot button issues as abortion, gay marriage, and stem cell research. Such a list signals that Conservative Christians have been able to set the agenda, while issues that Progressive Christians might care about like poverty, war, and the environment are sidelined. In addition, as discussed in earlier chapters, Conservatives have been able to frame much of the debate so that responsibility for many public issues is assigned to the individual American, rather than larger bodies like corporations or the government. Finally, the Conservatives have also narrowed the possible solutions so that expanding government programs is not a viable remedy to most existing problems.

All of this is not to say that the Democrats have been largely absent from the battleground of the frame wars. For instance, there continues to be a significant battle between the parties over who is to blame for rising healthcare costs. In truth, there are several contributing factors to the problem: insurance companies, pharmaceutical companies, patients, doctors and hospitals, government agencies, and lawyers. The Democrats want to rein in insurance companies and the pharmaceutical industry, believing their marketing expenditures and high profit margins are to blame for the rising costs. If they are successful in framing the issue in this way, they can pass legislation to regulate these industries, offering some government intervention as a viable solution to the problem. Republicans, on the other hand, want to rein in the trial lawyers, believing that their aggressive pursuit of lawsuits hurts business and reduces innovation. This frame allows them to suggest a solution, which would put caps on lawsuit awards and limit where and how people can bring claims against companies. These competing frames were showcased in the 2004 Vice-Presidential debate:

"My concern is specifically with what's happened to our medical care system because of rising malpractice insurance rates, because we failed to adequately reform our medical liability structure. I was in New Mexico the other day and met with a group of OB/GYN docs. And they were deeply concerned because they were fearful that there'd be another increase in malpractice insurance rates as a result of what they believe are frivolous lawsuits and that that would put them out of business.... We passed medical liability reform through the House of Representatives. It's been blocked in the Senate. Senator Kerry's voted 10 times against medical liability reform, and I don't believe Senator Edwards supports it, either, not the kind that would be meaningful." – Dick Cheney, October 5th, 2004

"Well let me say, first of all, I'm proud of the work I did on behalf of kids and families against big insurance companies, big drug companies and big HMOs. We do have too many lawsuits. And the reality is there's something that we can do about it. But we don't believe that we should take away the right of people like Valerie Lakey, who was the young girl who I represented, five years old, severely injured for life, on a defective swimming pool drain cover. . We have a serious health care plan to bring down costs for everybody, to cover millions more Americans and to actually stand up to drug companies and insurance companies which this administration has been unwilling to do." – John Edwards, October 5th, 2004

As the above example demonstrates, there will always be opportunities for Democrats to influence how the public interprets specific issues. And yet, because we are playing catch-up, especially in terms of framing values, much of the framing work we must do will be in response to already existing frames created by the Republicans. While it is easier to frame than reframe, the rhetorical work of previous persuaders, namely Conservatives, have predisposed many members of the audience to view the world in ways that are out of line with a progressive agenda. As a result, Democrats will need to respond to pre-existing frames. Democrats must survey the context and decide in each specific instance how they want to operate given the particular circumstances. They have at least three options: try to align their frame with existing frames, counter those frames, or change them.

Working with Existing Frames

The simplest and most common approach to framing is to work with those frames the audience already accepts. In essence, this approach does not require the persuader to create new frames, but allows them to rely on the persuasive work done by others. The persuader merely needs to frame their message to fit the pre-existing frames of the audience. In aligning with existing frames, persuaders work to craft their message in terms of the audience's pre-existing interests, values, and beliefs. They can also highlight the ways in which their goals are in line with pre-existing cultural beliefs. Working with existing frames is often attractive because the persuader knows the audience will accept their message to some degree based on their acceptance of the underlying frames. While this is a common approach to framing, in the current context Progressive persuaders cannot gain much ground by using it. In fact, this approach is most frequently employed by those persuaders who don't understand how to challenge existing frames or lack the power to influence those frames in a meaningful way.

There can be little doubt that Democrats have been trying to advance persuasive appeals within pre-existing frames for the last several decades. This is in part because they were largely unaware of how framing was being used against them and in part because they greatly underestimated the power of this persuasion tool. While aligning with existing frames may be necessary for short-term gains or useful in certain instances, it can be quite harmful over time.

One of the greatest costs for Democrats is their loss of a distinct voice advocating for issues based on a value set that is their own. In essence, aligning with existing frames has neutered the Party. As the Republicans have been influencing the audience's values and constructing the cultural mandates, we've been forced to either withdraw some of our arguments from the public sphere or reframe them to such an extent they are no longer recognizable, greatly tempering our passion for expressing them. We have paid a high price for taking the worn path.

Perhaps the most striking and most damaging example of this can be found in Bill Clinton's adoption of Reagan's anti-government rhetoric. Throughout his two terms in office, Clinton often used this frame to position himself as a fiscal moderate who was in line with the current ways of thinking in American society. For example, in his 1996 radio address to the nation he declared, "The era of big government is over" and then described how he would trim programs. In conforming to and using anti-government frames, Clinton was able to make short-term gains and garner support from Americans. Unfortunately this came at a cost to Progressive ideals, which encourage a central role for effective and efficient government.

Creating Counter Frames[11]

Another, more proactive approach to framing is the creation of counter frames. Counter frames are often seen as a defensive tool in persuasion because they are crafted in response to the opposition's deployment of successful frames. Persuaders create counter frames to reduce the rhetorical power of the opposition, while at the same time increasing their own potential to gain the audience's attention. As a result, persuaders working with counter frames must be able to not only contest the original frame, but also offer an alternative perspective for the public to consider.

Political persuaders typically use counter-framing techniques when they openly challenge their opposition, particularly in terms of their credibility. There are two primary techniques used in this vein, each of which bears closer consideration:

Vilification

Vilification is used by a persuader to cast doubt on the way her opponent has framed herself and her policies. This strategy attempts to reveal the various ways in which the opposition is working against the interests of the audience, thereby using contrast to place the persuader on the moral high ground. One interesting approach here has been by Conservative legislators who have often used this tactic when they portray homosexuals in the debate over gay marriage. Typically, they vilify homosexuals, claiming they are attacking the traditional culture in their demands for equal rights. This allows the Conservatives to play the role of victim, rather than the aggressors.

In the 2004 election, both Kerry and Bush created counter frames as they tried to demonstrate how their opponent

---

[11] McCaffrey & Keys, 2000

did not have the interest of the average American at heart. Bush's primary challenges to Kerry's frame centered on economic issues, particularly spending. As Kerry worked to construct himself as fiscally responsible, Bush attempted to vilify him on this front. For example, in one campaign piece, voters were told, "John Kerry has proposed at least $1.9 trillion in new government spending. He says he will pay for it by taxing the rich, but he will have to raise taxes on all Americans to pay for his spending promises." Kerry also chose economic issues to vilify President Bush with the greatest emphasis on the favoritism he displayed towards America's wealthiest taxpayers. As one brochure notes, "George Bush has given tax breaks to the wealthiest Americans. In the coming decade, Bush will slash taxes for the wealthiest 1 percent of taxpayers by $758 billion." Here, Kerry works to strip Bush of his populist image by showing his real support is for upper class Americans.

Frame Debunking

Frame debunking is used by persuaders to highlight and discredit claims made by their opposition. In doing this, the persuader can challenge the public's previous acceptance of such claims, casting doubt on the opposition's character and motivations. One way to debunk existing frames is to highlight the opposition's inconsistencies either within the frame or between what they say and what they do.

In the 2004 presidential debates, both candidates focused on debunking various claims the other had made. Most often this was done by repeating what the opponent said and then contrasting it to other comments or past actions. Here are some examples of this tactic:

"Six months after he said Osama bin Laden must be caught dead or alive, this president was asked, 'Where is Osama bin Laden?' He said, 'I don't know. I don't really think about him very much. I'm not that concerned.' We need a president who stays deadly focused on the real war on terror." -John Kerry, October 13th, 2004

"He's just not credible when he talks about being fiscally conservative. He's just not credible. If you look at his record in the Senate, he voted to break the caps—the spending caps—over 200 times. And here he says he's going to be a fiscal conservative, all of a sudden. It's just not credible. You cannot believe it. And of course he's going to raise your taxes. You see, he's proposed $2.2 trillion of new spending. And you say: Well, how are you going to pay for it? He says, well, he's going to raise the taxes on the rich—that's what he said—the top two brackets. That raises, he says $800 billion; we say $600 billion. Now, either he's going to break all these wonderful promises he's told you about or he's going to raise taxes. And I suspect, given his record, he's going to raise taxes." -George Bush, October 13th, 2004

This tactic is even more effective if the debunking comes from an unexpected source. In politics this often happens when someone from within the party points out inconsistencies on the part of their own colleague. In the 2004 election, Zell Miller, a Democrat, also tried to debunk Kerry's claims during the campaign:

"Listing all the weapon systems that Senator Kerry tried his best to shut down sounds like an auctioneer selling off our national security but Americans need to know the facts. The B-1 bomber, that Senator Kerry opposed, dropped 40 percent of the bombs in the first six months of Operation Enduring Freedom.... Twenty years of votes can tell you much more about a man than twenty weeks of campaign rhetoric." -Zell Miller, September 1st, 2004

Counter framing can be an effective tool in political persuasion if used correctly. It is important, however, not to fall into the trap of relying solely on this defensive approach. Similar to pointing the finger in argument, this strategy inadvertently

69

highlights the frames of the opposition and can leave little space to advance new frames. The tactic works to create doubt in the mind of your audience, but this is not enough. A persuader rarely has both the time and the audience's attention to offer a viable alternative to the opposition they have effectively countered. With this in mind, Progressives cannot allow counter framing to substitute for the more difficult and long-term work of crafting new frames. As was suggested earlier and many of us know all too well, we cannot win elections solely on the merits of our critique.

Changing Frames

The most difficult (and most rewarding) approach to framing is the creation of new frames. As Lakoff points out, changing frames is a long-term process, which involves deep analysis of the current rhetorical landscape, testing and choosing language to match the desired frame, and consistent deployment of the frames in simple language that resonates with the intended audience. In trying to change frames, persuaders must recognize that the framing process is at work on a variety of levels. It is rarely sufficient to change the language around a particular issue. Instead, persuaders must work to change framing at the deeper levels that impact how we think and act. Lawrence Wallack (2005) offers a succinct explanation of how Lakoff's three levels of analysis work:

At *Level One,* people analyze the information they are given in terms of the widely shared values of the society in which they live. These values, even as they are generally agreed upon, are often ambiguous, allowing different people to interpret them in vastly different ways.

While there are many values found at this level, some of which may even be in conflict with one another, persuaders will work to limit the number of values we consider, as well as direct the ways in which we interpret them. For example, as Americans, we might value both community and self-reliance. But a persuader who wishes to set our frames may consistently backdrop the value of community and highlight self-reliance in their persuasive appeals. Alternatively, the persuader might present the value of community, but suggest an interpretation of it that includes neighborhood picnics, but not government supported community centers.

At *Level Two,* people try to decide what type of issue is being discussed, trying to classify or categorize it. Some potential categories include political issues, moral issues, and economic issues.

Persuaders are actively trying to influence the classification of a given issue because they recognize how we classify an issue may very well determine our response to that issue. For example, religious conservatives who supported Bush in the 2004 election framed the election as a moral one for their audience. People who did not vote were ignoring their moral responsibility, thereby allowing the morally corrupt to set the agenda. In addition, the Religious Right sought to limit what issues were classified as moral concerns. They repeatedly focused on abortion and gay marriage, directing their audience's attention to these moral issues. In contrast, they did not speak about poverty, social services, war, or the environment. These issues were backdropped and, therefore, exempt from moral classification.

At *Level Three,* people analyze solutions to tangible problems, often in terms of particular policies.

At this level persuaders are typically focused on tying specific terms to specific policies. They will seek language that positively frames the policies they support and negatively frames the policies they do not. To be successful, the terminology must

71

be deployed early enough to repeatedly disseminate it. It must work to activate the intended frame in the mind of the target audience. In the last election, both sides tried to deploy terms that framed the issues in their favor. A term that became infamous in the election was *flip-flopper*. The term *flip-flopper* was deployed during the election for a very specific purpose: to create doubt around John Kerry's credibility. Because voters were largely unaware of who John Kerry was, the Republicans worked diligently to create, disseminate, and highlight one term that would effectively frame him in a negative light. Recognizing that the American people valued strength, stability, and consistency (especially during a time of war), they used *flip-flopper* to encapsulate weakness and inconsistency.

The Democrats also tried to find terminology that would frame certain issues in ways that were rhetorically beneficial to them. One of the terms that gained some traction, but was ultimately not very effective was *backdoor draft*. While this term has elements that clearly work to paint the stop-gap policy in a negative light, the policy itself is quite complex and unknown to many Americans. Most Americans had never considered the issue prior to the election, meaning that they had not yet framed it at Level One or Level Two. Because the Democrats were never able to fully explain how the stop-gap policy itself worked or the ways in which it was similar to a draft, they were unable to harness the power of the term *backdoor draft*.

Many analysts, including Lakoff himself, have suggested that Democrats are having trouble with their persuasion because they have spent the last several decades focused on Level Three debates, while the Republicans have been quietly working on the values at Level One. Controlling the frames at Level One is similar to constructing a society's common knowledge. Once you have framed people's values, you are able to easily frame the issues. As suggested above, framing at Level One is of great benefit to the persuader because it reduces the rhetorical work they need to do at the other levels. In addition, it makes it more difficult for the opposition to gain ground with their messages.

The Framing of Politics

The Republicans' successful framing techniques rely on three things: 1) a consistent message coming from a variety of voices, 2) discipline in staying on message, and 3) commitment to constant repetition of the message. Their success means that we have much damage to undo. We will need to begin our work by challenging existing Level One frames. Once these frames have been sufficiently destabilized, we will need to shift our focus to disseminating Progressive frames, which highlight a new set of values in the minds of everyday Americans.

One of the major changes we need to seek through our reframing is a commitment on the part of all Americans to work towards a society that is accountable to all its citizens. This frame would replace the overriding frame of personal responsibility that has dominated the culture for the last 25 years. Our new frame would push back on the Conservative's commitment to the individual which has encouraged Americans to view themselves as outside of the social contract and not responsible for others. Such framing would begin at the value level of community, work to classify more issues as social ones rather than economic or private issues, and depend on phrases such as *the common good* and *the public good*.

Better Persuasion: 3 Things You Can Do

1) Use language that assumes and promotes the value of the *public good*.

The process of rewriting much of our common knowledge or societal assumptions is a long term one. Much of the decision-making regarding re-framing must happen at the national level in order to build upon credible research and create consistency in messaging. But every Progressive can start reframing our society's foundational values in terms of the *public good* in small ways. Survey the current context for opportunities that allow you to practice your reframing. Seize upon powerful national stories like the response to Hurricane Katrina. Use it to highlight the value of the public good in everyday exchanges with the people around you. By framing your message with language that assumes your fellow Americans value the public good, you can make several arguments. For instance:

- Because we want all members of our society to be free from uncertainty and have some safety net in the case of unforeseen misfortune like Hurricane Katrina, we cannot cut funding for important programs like Medicare and Medicaid.
- Because we value our elderly population and believe they should be rewarded for the work they did in their earlier years, we must protect Social Security.
- Because this country has always valued the preservation of exceptional places like Yosemite, the Grand Canyon, and the Everglades, we need to continue this legacy and protect our natural landscape so that it will be available for future generations of Americans to enjoy

2) Use specific existing frames to our advantage.

While Progressives have largely been hurt by their reliance on existing frames, there are times when these frames can be used to our advantage. In relying on existing frames, make sure to choose those frames which offer Progressives more benefit than harm. One such example would be the framing of the term radical:

- *Radical* – Most Americans have been trained to believe that radicalism is inherently disruptive and therefore poses a threat to them and the stability of their lives. Progressive should consistently talk about right-wing Republicans as *radicals*, pointing out how they would like to radically alter American culture. The term Right-wing Radical is not only catchy, it is also quite useful. Examples of radical actions you can highlight include attacking another country without provocation, removing the wall

between church and state, and rolling back many forms
of privacy protections.

3) Build frames at the grassroots level.

While there will be much work done at the national level, there
are a whole host of important campaigns closer to home. If you
are working on a campaign in your area, try to find frames that
will effectively resonate with your target audiences. One of the
best ways to create consistency across the campaign is to
disseminate the messages you want people to repeat. These *talking
points*, which lie at the heart of the Republican rhetorical strategy,
create simple and consistent messages the media will use and the
public will become familiar with – coming to think in the terms
you use. In grassroots campaigns, it is a good idea to use e-mail
lists to spread the word regarding specific framing techniques.
Such an approach activates the power of interpersonal networks
as the first step in getting the message out.

CHAPTER 5

STRAIGHT TO THE HEART

One of the great ironies for Progressives is that they are often noted for their bleeding hearts, but generally shy away from making emotional arguments in the political sphere. This is because when it comes to persuasion, Democrats generally feel more at home with logical appeals than emotional ones. This tendency is unfortunate because emotional appeals are almost always more effective at eliciting action from an audience. Such appeals gain their potency from targeting the feelings of the audience which allows the persuader to create a sense of intimacy and build relationships. This intimacy encourages the audience to trust the persuader and do as he or she suggests. Motivational appeals are the most common persuasion techniques in our society today, found throughout advertising, entertainment, and, increasingly, the news media. Persuaders favor such appeals for a number of reasons: 1) they are easier to communicate, 2) they are more difficult to challenge, 3) they persuade more quickly, 4) they are oriented towards action or behavioral change, and 5) they effectively influence high-risk decision-making.

Political persuaders have long understood the power of motivational appeals. Some of the most well-known American political leaders, including Abraham Lincoln, Teddy Roosevelt, JFK, and Bill Clinton, have been regarded as masters of such appeals. These leaders used their persuasion not only to influence ideas and attitudes, but also to successfully encourage the public to act upon those ideas, even when doing so involved great sacrifice or tremendous change. Because of their power to move people to action, motivational appeals are a key tool for political persuaders. As Democrats discovered with the youth vote in the

76

last election, it is not enough for people to think that one candidate is better than another; they must also act on that belief and vote. In addition, if we are to build a grassroots political movement to reclaim this country, we must do more than vote, we must motivate other Progressives to become much more politically active.

Effective motivational appeals evoke various emotions, respond to psychological needs, and utilize cultural values. Having previously explored the role of culture and the importance of cultural values, this chapter will focus on appealing to emotions and needs.

Emotions

Emotions guide how we understand our feelings and how we organize our reactions to those feelings. Over time, we come to recognize what various emotions mean and develop patterns of response to those emotions. When confronted with information during decision-making, people often let their emotions guide their behavior by giving more weight to how they feel than what they think. People also tend to see their own emotional experience as more valid than facts and figures. This is the case even though such responses are typically ambiguous and difficult to explain.

Political persuaders often rely on emotional appeals for the simple reason that such appeals work, and work quickly. Emotional appeals bypass logic and go straight for the heart, thereby quickly producing the desired action. In addition, a political persuader can benefit from such a response because the audience does not demand the more complex arguments associated with logical appeals. The result is not only simpler messages, but also the opportunity to impact a broader audience who may process reasons and argument differently, but whose emotional responses might be quite similar. In political

77

persuasion there are several key emotions that persuaders primarily appeal to: pride, fear, guilt, and hope.[12]

Pride
When a person feels pride, he experiences a sense of self-worth based on his own achievements or the achievements of others he is associated with. People can express pride in their company, their family, or even their hometown football team. They also express pride in terms of their nationality. When someone says, "I'm proud to be an American," he is articulating a feeling of national pride or patriotism. This pride is often based upon a sense of value he attaches to such things as the American way of life, various choices available in America, and American history.

Pride is an important tool for political persuaders in a democracy because political leaders must gain the public's favor as they pursue their agenda. In this context, pride is valuable because persuaders can evoke it to gain support and quell opposition. In contemporary American culture, persuaders invoke pride primarily by linking feelings of patriotism to the notion of duty. In essence, patriotism is presented as the duty to stand with one's country. This duty is encapsulated in the bumper sticker: "America: Love It or Leave It." Thus, "patriotic" Americans do their duty by supporting their country, and those who do not fully support the country should not reside within its borders. Many Americans easily extend this approach to national pride when they claim that patriotic Americans support their government's foreign policy agenda and do not question the sacrifices it may entail, including war and censorship.

George Bush often evokes a sense of duty in his rhetoric concerning our current wars in the Middle East:

---

[12] Humor is another type of appeal, but unlike fear or guilt, which persuade directly, humor works in a more circular manner. Humor serves to capture attention, divert attention, and increase liking for the persuader. While it is a popular appeal with Progressives, it is often less effective than more direct emotional appeals.

"We're being challenged like never before. And we have a duty to our country and to future generations of America to achieve a free Iraq, a free Afghanistan, and to rid the world of weapons of mass destruction." -George Bush, September 30th, 2004

Such duty relies on a simple but powerful set of assumptions: America is a united entity with a single motive and voice, America is always striving for the ideal, and American leaders should be given the benefit of the doubt by their citizens. These assumptions, widely held by Americans, label critique and dissent as unpatriotic, reject difference based on the fear of division, and often require us to favor an independent America over an America that works together with other nations.

Recognizing the power of patriotism, every Democrat should be alarmed at the Republicans' successful hijacking of national pride. Like many trends discussed in this book, the cause can be attributed to the rhetorical choices of both the Republicans and the Democrats. For their part, Republicans have consistently reached out to voters, especially Southern voters, through an appeal to patriotism that in essence asserted, "America is the best." This simple appeal offered a strong sense of identity and purpose, as well as a clear rallying point in support of the military and a nostalgic sense of American life. Republicans extended their appeals based on national pride following September 11th. The appeals to patriotism offered safety and a sense of belonging to a shocked and fearful nation. Such appeals were also used to frame the Administration's decision to ignore the UN's ruling and go to Iraq War as a move of independence rather than arrogance.

The Democrats, on the other hand, have been on a steady retreat from the language of patriotism for the last several decades. We have questioned and clearly rejected the Republican version of patriotism, which sounds arrogant and combative. But instead of crafting our own powerful approach to national pride, we have offered only mild dissent, often in a defensive tone, or have opted to embrace a type of globalism as a backdrop to

American nationalism. For example, in the first presidential debate Kerry continually referred to the importance of *strong alliances, reaching out, make it so America isn't doing this alone.* In contrast, Bush kept focused on the *nation's duty, our will, protecting our children and grandchildren.*

The Progressive's decision to retreat from this powerfully persuasive ground is too costly. We must craft our own version of national pride, which speaks to the average American, while at the same time highlighting noble American characteristics and encouraging moral leadership in international affairs. Barack Obama offers a good example of this patriotism in his speech at the 2004 Democratic National Convention. Here he appeals to national pride based on our ideals rather than the values typically fore fronted by Republicans:

"Tonight, we gather to affirm the greatness of our Nation, not because of the height of our skyscrapers, or the power of our military, or the size of our economy. Our pride is based on a very simple premise, summed up in a declaration made over two hundred years ago: 'We hold these truths to be self-evident, that all men are created equal, and they are endowed by their Creator with certain inalienable rights, that among these are Life, Liberty and the pursuit of Happiness'." -Barack Obama, July 26th, 2004

Fear
One of the most basic human emotions is fear. Fear is generally understood as either a response to a specific danger or a more ambiguous sense of being frightened about potential events. People often feel fear when they are confronted with uncertainty or lack the ability to control their environment. Most research on fear and persuasion suggests that the more fear a persuader uses in their appeal, the more likely that appeal will be effective. This is because the more fear aroused in an audience, the more that audience feels vulnerable and therefore the more willing they are to accept the remedy suggested. Research also indicates that for fear appeals to work, audience members must see the suggested remedy as both effective and feasible. As a result, fear appeals

must be coupled with quick and easy solutions. A persuader cannot continue to benefit from fear appeals over a long period of time without following through on the proposed solution.

Throughout history, political persuaders have relied on the power of fear to bypass reason and secure adherence to their messages. Given that fear is such a negative state, people often react to it without thinking. This can be the case even when the specific threat is unclear. Not only does ambiguity allow the persuader to increase fear, it also allows the persuader to extend a sense of threat from one source to many others. This was clearly done by the Republicans when they linked September 11th to the Iraq War and the potential election of Kerry with future attacks:

"We are now acting because the risks of inaction would be far greater. In one year, or five years, the power of Iraq to inflict harm on all free nations would be multiplied many times over. With these capabilities, Saddam Hussein and his terrorist allies could choose the moment of deadly conflict when they are strongest. We choose to meet that threat now, where it arises, before it can appear suddenly in our skies and cities." -George Bush, March 18th, 2003

"We're now at that point where we're making that kind of decision for the next 30 or 40 years, and it's absolutely essential that eight weeks from today, on November 2nd, we make the right choice. Because if we make the wrong choice, then the danger is that we'll get hit again, that we'll be hit in a way that will be devastating from the standpoint of the United States, and that we'll fall back into the pre-9/11 mind set if you will, that in fact these terrorist attacks are just criminal acts, and that we're not really at war. I think that would be a terrible mistake for us."
-Dick Cheney, September 7th, 2004

While both parties used fear appeals during the 2004 election, Democrats were generally more subtle and varied in their suggested threats. Some of these threats included economic instability, North Korea, and even George Bush himself. In fact one popular bumper sticker read: "Defend America: Defeat

Bush." The Republicans, on the other hand, were much more direct in their fear appeals, primarily encouraging a fear of terrorism. Threats from terrorists were highlighted both indirectly and directly in the months leading up to the election through such tactics as the declaration of orange alerts and suggestions that the election might have to be postponed due to terrorist threats. These fear appeals consistently reminded the public of the potential for attack. In addition, many Republican candidates for office and their advocates directly rekindled thoughts of the September 11th attack as they campaigned in 2004. In the final assessment, the Republicans' use of fear appeals during the 2004 election was more effective simply because the threat they highlighted was clearer, simpler, and more believable to the American public based on recent experience.

After the 2004 election, however, as shifts in context and priorities occurred, other threats gained more potency. For example, the Democrats were able to successfully use fear appeals around another issue, Social Security:

"Let me share with you why I believe the president's plan is so dangerous. The Bush plan would take our already record-high $4.3 trillion national debt and put us another $2 trillion in the red. That's an immoral burden to place on the backs of the next generation. But maybe most of all, the Bush plan isn't really Social Security reform; it's more like Social Security roulette. Democrats are all for giving Americans more of a say and more choices when it comes to their retirement savings, but that doesn't mean taking Social Security's guarantee and gambling with it. And that's coming from a senator who represents Las Vegas." -Harry Reid, February 2nd, 2005

These appeals effectively reduced support for Bush's plan and derailed his policy objectives on this issue. As the context changed, the potential for fear appeals around domestic issues increased.

82

Guilt

Guilt is a negative emotional state that occurs when a person feels like she's violating societal norms or her own individual conscience. Like other emotional appeals, persuaders typically use guilt to encourage a change of behavior. Research suggests guilt works. People are more likely to comply with requests when a sense of guilt has been provoked. In addition, studies show that successful guilt appeals are crafted in terms of the positive feelings of doing the desirable action rather than the negative feelings of refraining from the undesirable action.
Political persuaders frequently use guilt to encourage allegiance and reduce opposition. They also use such appeals not only to solidify adherence to particular societal norms, but also to elicit specific actions. In campaigns, guilt is often used to encourage voting. Potential voters are told that staying away from the polls ignores the sacrifice made by others to ensure a true democracy. In this last election, Democrats primarily used guilt appeals to turn young voters out to vote. Republicans, on the other hand, focused their guilt appeals on religious voters. Many Republicans within the conservative Christian movement urged their fellow believers to vote by sponsoring such campaigns as "Value Your Vote and Vote Your Values," reminding religious voters that they were neglecting their duty as citizens and Christians when they did not cast their ballots. For example, Cedar Park Pastor Joseph Fuiten told members of his congregation:

"In these days of very close elections, every vote counts. And it's very important for every person to vote. We want religious people to be active in the vote this year. This is a very important year for the religious vote.. Christian citizens should be involved. It's a crime when they're not." -Rev. Joseph Fuiten, August 27th, 2004

At times during the 2004 election, the Republican guilt appeals extended beyond the goal of getting religious voters out on election day. This was particularly true in appeals targeted at Catholics, a key swing constituency. Several American bishops made national news when they suggested that Catholics could not cast a vote for John Kerry in good conscience. Again, such appeals are successful because the bishops framed the moral issues for their audience and then directed their behavior.

While both parties appealed to guilt throughout the campaign, the key difference was the nature of their audiences. Arguably, young voters were unlikely to be affected by guilt appeals, as they are in a period of their development where they are aggressively seeking to assert their independence. On the other hand, religious voters were easier targets for such appeals as they are more conditioned and vulnerable to the emotion of guilt as it is a common theme in much religious discourse.

Hope
Hope, or the belief that some promise will be fulfilled, is a powerful emotion in the human condition. Hope sustains people under even the direst conditions and can offer support in the pursuit of difficult to reach goals. While hope is central to many uplifting motivational appeals, political persuaders exploit the emotion for specific reasons. First, unlike appeals to fear or guilt, appeals to hope offer the audience overtly positive incentives for action. In situations where people may have grown apathetic, depressed, or overwhelmed, political persuaders can craft hopeful appeals that invigorate listeners to act for change. Second, appeals to hope allow the persuader to highlight problems while maintaining a positive perspective, thereby enacting the optimism that is part of American culture.

One of the most memorable appeals crafted around hope was former President Clinton's oft references to his hometown of Hope, Arkansas. He effectively constructed both his personal narrative and his vision for America using the emotional appeal of hope. Hope was the central component of a narrative which not only highlighted his own humble beginnings, but also encouraged Americans to believe in and work towards a brighter future.

Because hope is such a strong ideal, political persuaders may also target emotions by accusing their opponent of taking hope away. Bush and Kerry sparred over hope on a variety of occasions, with each trying to suggest that the other was creating a less hopeful society. While Bush primarily accused Kerry of instilling a sense of hopelessness around the Iraq War, Kerry made the same accusations about specific domestic policies. For example, in discussing stem cell research Kerry recalled:

"I was at a forum with Michael J. Fox the other day in New Hampshire, who's suffering from Parkinson's, and he wants us to do stem cell, embryonic stem cell. And this fellow stood up, and he was quivering. His whole body was shaking from the nerve disease, the muscular disease that he had. And he said to me and to the whole hall, he said 'You know, don't take away my hope, because my hope is what keeps me going'." -John Kerry, October 8th, 2004

In the 2004 election, Democrats based much of their presidential campaign on hope. In fact one of the key phrases used by Kerry was "Hope is on the way." While this phrase was, at first glance, a good rhetorical choice, it ended up being somewhat problematic. First, it became part of a largely defensive campaign responding to the Republicans' assertion that Kerry's constant critique of the Bush Administration made him a pessimist. Because it was defensive in nature, the authentic optimism of such an appeal was largely reduced. Second, in the post September 11th context, fear appeals resonated more deeply with the American public and were therefore more effective. It was simply too soon and the outlook was too ambiguous for Americans to be truly hopeful. This was made worse by the fact that Kerry's recovery plan was difficult to follow and therefore difficult to believe in. While hope will always have a place in political persuasion, in the future Democrats need to survey the context before deciding whether this emotional appeal should be a central component of their campaigns. As September 11th continues to fade, hope may once again be an effective appeal.

Needs

Human beings have various needs they are motivated to fulfill in order to reduce stress and feel satisfaction. One of the most familiar and useful models of needs is found in Maslow's Hierarchy (1943). Maslow presents the hierarchy of needs in a pyramid, suggesting that our basic needs, those at the foundation of the pyramid, must be fulfilled before we are motivated by higher level needs. While it is easy to see the model as linear, it is important to remember that for any given person these needs emerge and recede over time and depend largely on context.

Political persuaders seek to demonstrate how their policy or candidate will better fulfill a range of audience needs. The effective persuader is keenly aware of how the particularities of an audience and the specifics of context determine which needs he should highlight in his appeal. Some audiences will be grappling with more basic needs as a result of their economic conditions, while others will be more interested in fulfilling higher-level needs like love and belonging. In the same vein, context may allow a persuader to effectively appeal to higher-level needs such as esteem or self-actualization in times of peace and prosperity, while more tumultuous contexts require messages that focus on fulfilling safety needs. The persuader must analyze the audience and the situation before choosing to focus on a particular need. Below each of these needs is explored beginning with the most basic need and moving to the highest level need:

Physiological/basic needs—the need for food, clothing, shelter, sleep, and physical health

In contemporary American culture most people's basic needs are fulfilled. Even in the worst of economic times, the credit system and some remaining government programs can keep people afloat. As a result, American political persuaders are generally not very successful in appealing to basic needs. The one important exception to this rule is the emerging health care crisis.

In the 2004 election some Democrats, particularly at the state level, were able to successfully focus their campaigns on this issue, offering their innovative policies and their leadership as a partial solution to the problem. Because health care appeals to voters in terms of their most basic needs, Democrats need to make this a key issue in all state and federal campaigns in the near future. As the health care crisis worsens, Americans across the board will become more and more interested in having the need for quality health care met.

Security and Safety needs—the need for a sense of stability and freedom from physical danger

Prior to September 11th, most Americans thought about safety needs primarily in terms of economic stability and safety from crime. After the attack, security needs were filtered through a lens of terrorist threat. Even those Americans living in states like Nebraska, which were unlikely targets for future terrorist attacks, felt vulnerable just because they were Americans. This vulnerability or need for security was heightened by much of the pre-election rhetoric in 2004. Republicans appealed to safety needs primarily because they believed they were stronger on terrorism than Democrats. They created campaign materials that continually portrayed their candidates as steadfast and resolute, people who would protect America, particularly by staying on the offensive. George Bush embodied this approach in the first debate when he said: "My attitude is, you take preemptive action in order to protect the American people, that you act in order to make this country secure." In addition, Republicans successfully argued that Democrats, and particularly John Kerry, would be unable to offer such protection because of a tendency towards inconsistency and indecision. In that same debate, Bush claimed Kerry's inconsistency would hurt our potential for alliances when he said, "They're not going to follow somebody who says this is the wrong war at the wrong place at the wrong time. They're not going to follow somebody whose core convictions keep changing because of politics in America."

Social needs—the need to be loved, to be accepted, and to belong

Many of the appeals made during the 2004 election emphasized the need to belong, specifically to belong to the national community. This desire coincided directly with the need to feel secure, as people saw their safety in association with other Americans following September 11th. As John McCain articulated at the RNC Convention:

"In that moment, we were not different races. We were not poor or rich. We were not Democrat or Republican, liberal or conservative. We were not two countries. We were Americans. All of us, despite the differences that enliven our politics, are united in the one big idea that freedom is our birthright and its defense is always our first responsibility." -John McCain, August 30th, 2004

After the initial response of unifying began to fade and break down, there was a call on many fronts for the country to act like it was still united. This call was most succinctly embodied in the phrase "United We Stand," which appeared on bumper stickers and ribbons across the nation. Many Americans sought to unify America, believing not only that stronger ties would make them feel more secure, but also that a united country was likely to be less vulnerable to attack.

Because social needs were so important in the eyes of many Americans during the 2004 election, political persuaders from both parties keyed on unity during their campaigns. Such appeals were especially important for the presidential candidates, as national leaders are often expected to bring the country together. The need for belonging and association proved to be difficult rhetorical ground for the Democrats. They were put in the awkward position of using division to gain the critical edge they needed to effectively oppose President Bush, while simultaneously trying to fulfill the American voter's pressing need for unity. While Democrats often tried unsuccessfully to walk this line, most Republicans chose to act like the country *was* united. Specifically, they portrayed the American people as united in their resolve against foreign enemies.

But again as context changes, opportunities change. As September 11th receded in prominence and other concerns arose, the need to belong, to be a part of something, could be articulated in ways that were more advantageous to Progressives. For example, following Hurricane Katrina and the Bush Administration's botched response, Senator Kerry's appeal to belonging resonated much more effectively:

"Rarely has there been a moment more urgent for Americans to step up and define ourselves again. On the line is a fundamental choice. A choice between a view that says 'you're on your own,' 'go it alone,' or 'every man for himself.' Or a different view—a different philosophy—a different conviction of governance—a belief that says our great American challenge is one of shared endeavor and shared sacrifice." -John Kerry, September 19th, 2005

Esteem needs—the need to be valued, to be appreciated, and to be wanted

In the area of political persuasion, the need for self-esteem is frequently tied to patriotism. Most Americans want to feel like their country is valued and that their citizenship is something others respect or even envy. Prior to our invasion of Iraq, there were clear indications that other nations disagreed with our policy and were voicing disappointment with our nation. This feeling became even more acute after no weapons of mass destruction were found, reports that Iraqi civilian deaths were mounting, contracts were being awarded to politically connected corporations like Halliburton, and scandals like the torture of prisoners at Abu Ghraib were coming to light.

Over time, many Americans began to feel uneasy and needed reassurance that the country was doing the right thing and would be judged as right in their course of action. This need was very difficult for Democrats to fulfill because we were primarily concerned about our international image and reputation. Most Democrats looked at world opinion and found very little comfort there. Republicans, on the other hand, didn't really focus on what other countries thought of America. In fact, Bush often liked to point out that he was committed to being right, not popular, on the world scene:

"People love America. Sometimes they don't like decisions made by America, but I don't think you want a president who tries to become popular and does the wrong thing." – George Bush, October 8th, 2004

Self-actualization needs—the need to achieve one's fullest potential

Similar to esteem needs in this case, the last election appealed to self-actualization needs primarily in terms of America's role as a chosen nation. After claims of WMDs in Iraq proved false, many Americans grappled with a legitimate purpose for the war. The Bush Administration met this need by offering a simple and believable claim tying the war to the duty of America to spread freedom throughout the world. This easy explanation also served to reduce critique of our foreign policy in the Middle East as Republicans explained our attack as part of a larger plan to spread freedom in that region. This sense of purpose is illustrated in John Thune's comments in a NBC News' Meet the Press debate with Tom Daschle in 2004:

"I think we have to continue to try and build a broader coalition of support from those nations around the world who care about freedom, like this country does. We decided to move against Iraq, tried to involve the international community, got some support, trying to build a broader coalition as we move forward when it comes to stabilizing Iraq and providing a democracy and a freedom there that will provide stability in that region of the world." -John Thune, September 19th, 2004

Republicans like Thune easily honed in on self-actualization needs. In contrast, Democrats were once again put in the difficult position of being unwilling to make these same claims, but also unable to critique the appeals used by Republicans.

Better Persuasion: 3 Things You Can Do

1) Craft motivational appeals with a populist flavor that appeal to the emotions of hope and indignation.

William Blake once wrote, "The voice of honest indignation is the voice of God." Indignation has a powerful place in Progressive rhetoric. While it is not heard very often, it is remarkable when it appears. One of the most attractive aspects of Howard Dean's appeals was the authenticity tied to his indignation. Dean resonated with so many Americans, particularly young Americans, because he was not afraid to speak his mind or demand answers. Most importantly, he did not do this from a place of weakness, rather, from the power of his indignation. And yet, while indignation is potent, it is not enough. We need to be able to offer a viable and valuable alternative to the American people. Americans need the hope that comes with a bold new direction as well. Here are some examples of an effective Progressive rhetoric that incorporates both hope and indignation:

- "America has been sorely tested in this new century and yet our leaders have largely pretended it's business as usual. We need to take a hard and honest look at these past few years, so that we can move forward in a way that better reflects the aspirations of our citizens and communities."
- "America's leaders have failed their citizens, all the while acting as if nothing was wrong. We've got to be braver

than that. Americans can make this country great, if only their leaders would be strong enough to admit they needed some help."

- "By pretending that nothing is wrong, things have gotten worse. We have to be brave enough to change direction. The hope for the future of America lies within the hands of the average American who is willing to say I want to make this country better, for myself, for my children, for my community. It starts with me."

2) Articulate a patriotism that is positive and progressive.

In *Reason: Why Liberals Will Win the Battle for America*, Robert Reich talks about positive patriotism. He argues that Progressives can best craft a new national pride on the basis of their commitment to their fellow citizens. Positive patriotism is expressed, both in words and actions, in a commitment to liberty, tolerance for dissent, willingness to pay our fair share in taxes, and an interest in making sure that every American is given the opportunity to reach his or her potential. This is much more in line with how Americans wants to see themselves and their country. In addition, it is much more affirming to be for something rather than against everything. Every Progressive who wants to appeal to national pride on these bases should start getting the message out now. Go to websites such as Café Press (www.cafepress.com) and Art Apart (www.artapart.com) to make bumper stickers and T-shirts with sayings like these:

- Patriotism means paying taxes
- Patriotism means tolerating dissent
- Patriotism means helping your fellow American

3) Appeal to specific needs based on the contemporary political context.

There are three easy steps every Progressive can follow in appealing to the needs of average Americans:

1. Survey the context and assess which needs are currently motivating the audience in their decision-making.
2. Craft messages that highlight those needs.
3. Offer a simple and feasible solution that will satisfy those needs.

There is strong evidence to suggest that barring another catastrophic terrorist attack, health care issues will be a central concern in the coming elections. This is good news for Democrats, who are generally seen as more credible and innovative on this topic. With rising health care costs, a growing lack of insurance coverage for working Americans, and a reduction in social services that provide health care benefits, there can be no doubt that this issue will be on the minds of many voters. In addition, because it is an issue that affects average Americans and affects them in terms of their basic needs, health care has clear potential to motivate Americans. Every Democrat should find out which organizations are working on health care issues in their state. Make a pledge to volunteer for one of these organizations at least twice before the next election.

CHAPTER 6

CRAFTING CREDIBILITY

In striving to improve their persuasive skills, many people make the mistake of focusing solely on the creation of better messages. But there is another important tool that resides not in the message, but in the messenger himself. That tool is credibility. Put simply, credibility is the degree to which the audience finds a communicator believable. While credibility is an important tool for all Progressives to develop and use effectively, it is particularly important for political candidates and campaign workers on the front lines.

Naturally, many Democrats involved in campaigns consider themselves to be credible figures. They know the issues and care deeply about the people they wish to represent. But credibility is more complicated than that. Like the other tools discussed in this handbook, credibility depends on audience perception and context. As such, credibility does not refer to the type of person someone actually *is*, but rather who an audience *perceives* that person to be. For example, a person may know everything there is to know about gun laws, but if he is a spokesperson for the NRA addressing a group seeking to ban assault weapons, he is unlikely to be seen as credible. It is the audience's negative perception of his affiliations, and perhaps his moral character, that reduces his credibility in their eyes. On the other hand, the same person speaking in front of a group of handgun enthusiasts would be granted almost instant credibility based on the very same information that caused the other audience to reject him. In addition to audience perception, credibility depends on context. Former President Clinton is naturally seen by many as a credible speaker on Israeli-Palestinian relations, but may very well be dismissed as an inappropriate speaker on wine-making.

In essence, the persuader makes various communication choices in order to present herself in a positive manner, but the audience's perception of that persuader as credible ultimately depends on factors she cannot entirely control. As a result, effective persuaders must not only consider how they can enhance their credibility in order to appeal to the widest audience possible, but they must also be keenly aware of which audiences are likely to find them credible, and on which topics they may legitimately speak.

Credibility is generally crafted along two different lines. The first, *extrinsic credibility* refers to the credibility a speaker accumulates over time. Extrinsic credibility is often understood in terms of a speaker's reputation, or what an audience knows about the speaker prior to hearing his persuasive appeal. While persuaders build their extrinsic credibility over time, they can also inform or remind an audience of this credibility at various points throughout any given persuasive appeal. The second, *intrinsic credibility* is more immediate, referring to how an audience perceives the speaker during the appeal. A speaker who wishes to be seen as a credible figure has the opportunity to influence her audience's perception of her credibility both prior to and during the persuasive appeal.[13] While persuaders try to enhance their extrinsic and intrinsic credibility at different points in time, a closer look at how each works will demonstrate that their major components are quite similar.

---

[13] Effective persuaders use both extrinsic and intrinsic credibility. In some cases there is limited or no opportunity for the speaker to build extrinsic credibility as in the case of door-to-door canvassing on behalf of a candidate. Where this is the case, a persuader should quickly communicate a credible affiliation his audience might value before focusing on the opportunity to build credibility during the appeal.

Extrinsic credibility

Extrinsic credibility is the credibility a persuader constructs prior to the appeal. Such credibility can be gained through 1) the development of expertise, 2) demonstrations of strong moral character, and 3) legitimate affiliations/associations. Extrinsic credibility benefits the persuader by ensuring that a general audience will give him the benefit of the doubt at the start of his persuasive appeal.

Focusing on factors which signal extrinsic credibility is particularly important in politics because the audience will rarely know the speaker personally. As a result, credibility is much less stable and enduring. With this in mind, a persuader must be cognizant of the specific audience he is addressing during a presentation. He should give close consideration to the values and motivations of his audience when choosing which factors to highlight among several that could improve his extrinsic credibility. Many persuaders incorrectly assume that certain expertise or affiliations will contribute to their credibility regardless of the specific audience. This is typically untrue. While a degree from Harvard might increase your stature during a talk on a college campus, it may very well fall flat in a talk to blue-collar workers.

Extrinsic credibility is a key factor in contemporary political persuasion. In the current context with televised images building a sense of intimacy with political figures, the individual candidate has become more important than the party they are affiliated with. An audience's perception of a candidate can therefore have an even greater impact on voters than their actual political skill or policy positions. The centrality of credibility has led political persuaders to spend much of their time highlighting their own and challenging the credibility of their opponent. As Frank Luntz, a key Republican strategist, has suggested, the 2004 Presidential election essentially came down to a contest over character. Nowhere was this showcased more clearly than in the debates in which each candidate focused on key aspects of credibility.

Expertise

A person can enhance her extrinsic credibility by developing knowledge and skills in areas pertinent to her persuasive appeal. Expertise is often linked to the study of, or direct experience with, the issue at hand. The more experience and training the persuader has, the more the audience will tend to see her as an expert on the topic, and the more legitimacy they will grant her as she makes her persuasive appeals. This is one of several reasons that incumbents enjoy a rhetorical advantage when making their case for re-election: an incumbent can more easily demonstrate a high level of expertise in the office for which they are campaigning.

At times, an audience is already aware of the persuader's expertise, but in many cases they will have to be informed or reminded. Most campaign materials are specifically designed to serve this purpose. Such materials offer a short review for voters looking to gather information on the candidate. The same is true in public appearances where those introducing the candidate are often expected to detail the candidate's expertise. In their opening remarks, such speakers often summarize the candidate's background, striving to relate it to the issue at hand and the audience being addressed. When the speaker must introduce herself, she will typically give the audience the major highlights of her experience and background in the first few minutes. In both cases this information assures the audience that the speaker is worthy of their time and attention. Once the audience is willing to hear the appeal, the speaker often continues to reference her expertise, consistently building credibility into her message. As might be expected, both presidential candidates referenced their expertise during the 2004 debates:

"I believe I'm going to win, because the American people know I know how to lead. I've shown the American people I know how to lead."-George Bush, September 30th, 2004

97

"I have a record of fighting for fiscal responsibility. In 1985, I was one of the first Democrats–broke with my party. We balanced the budget in the 90s. We paid down the debt for two years." -John Kerry, October 8th, 2004

Both candidates also called into question the expertise of their opponent:

"I think it's important, since he talked about the Medicare plan, has he been in the United States Senate for 20 years? He has no record of reforming health care. No record at all. He introduced some 300 bills and he's passed 5. No record of leadership." -George Bush, October 13th, 2004

"Being lectured by the president on fiscal responsibility is a little bit like Tony Soprano talking to me about law and order in this country." -John Kerry, October 13th, 2004

In general, Bush and his team repeatedly reminded voters of the expertise he had gained while serving his first term in office. They highlighted the extraordinary context in which he served, while downplaying his actual performance. They simultaneously called into question Kerry's ability to lead both in terms of domestic issues and foreign relations. Even though Kerry may have been better equipped to handle the duties of the presidency, he was unable to convincingly present himself as someone prepared for the challenges of this new political era.

Character
A speaker is thought to have more credibility if he has demonstrated a strong moral character in his personal and public life. Some attributes of such character might include taking responsibility, putting the interests of others before your own interest or special interests, having integrity, and being honest in your dealings with others. In addition, conducting a clean

campaign with little negative advertising and few allegations can contribute to credibility in terms of character.

Character was a central issue in the 2004 presidential election. Each campaign depicted its candidate as possessing a strong moral character, while at the same time highlighting their opponent's myriad character flaws. First, each candidate attempted to convince the viewing public that he would bring a strong moral character to his leadership role, putting the American people's interests above all else.

"And like Franklin Roosevelt, I don't care whether an idea is a Republican idea or a Democrat idea. I just care whether it works for America and whether it is going to make us stronger." -John Kerry, October 13th, 2004

"I came to Washington to solve problems. I was deeply concerned about seniors having to choose between prescription drugs and food. So I led. And in 2006, our seniors will get a prescription drug coverage in Medicare." -George Bush, October 13th, 2004

While both candidates recognized the importance of asserting their own moral character, each spent much more time demonstrating why his opponent lacked such character. This was done both subtly and more overtly:

"I'll nevertheless tell you that I think he (Bush) has not been candid with the American people. Now, he misled the American people in his speech when he said we will plan carefully. They obviously didn't. He misled the American people when he said we'd go to war as a last resort. We did not go as a last resort. And most Americans know the difference. . Now, this has cost us deeply in the world. I believe that it is important to tell the truth to the American people.... And I believe that what we need is a fresh start, new credibility." -John Kerry, September 30th, 2004

"I think what is misleading is to say you can lead and succeed in Iraq if you keep changing your positions on this war. And he has. As the politics change, his positions change. And that is not how a Commander-in-Chief acts. -George Bush, September 30th, 2004

The previous quotes embody the key strategies each side used to build doubt about their opponent's character. The Democrats' primary strategy was to consistently point out several misleading statements by the Bush Administration. Kerry's campaign believed that highlighting these gaps would diminish Bush's claim to integrity and honesty. While initially this appears to be a strong approach, the complexity of the post-9/11 political landscape and the desire of fearful Americans to believe their leaders would protect them, reduced its effectiveness. On the other hand, the Republican approach was much simpler. In a time of great uncertainty, they labeled Kerry a flip-flopper, continually pointed out his inconsistencies, and suggested that they exemplified his poor character. One of the most effective examples of this approach was the Republicans' claim that Kerry changed his position on the War in Iraq multiple times. They honed in on this allegation and repeated their message over and over. In addition, the Republicans presented video footage that succinctly supplied evidence for their claim.

Affiliations
In addition to considering expertise and character, an audience also evaluates a persuader's credibility based on their affiliations and associations. In small group scenarios a speaker who is a member of the group is automatically granted credibility by association. When the audience does not know the speaker personally, the person is often evaluated by the company he keeps. This is why so many product marketers use well-known figures to sell their products. The marketers hope that the celebrity's positive image will add to the credibility of the product itself. For political candidates, extrinsic credibility is tied not only

to one's party, but also to family members[14], their larger social circle, and their supporters. Candidates must strike a balance between highlighting the fact that they can get things done through powerful associates and assuring voters that they identify with and are similar to average Americans. They also have to be careful about any potential negative affiliations that their opponent may use against them. Once again, both presidential candidates used the debates to highlight their positive affiliations, while underscoring their opponent's negative affiliations:

"(M)y opponent keeps mentioning John McCain, and I'm glad he did. John McCain is for me for president because he understands I have the right view in winning the war on terror and that my plan will succeed in Iraq. And my opponent has got a plan of retreat and defeat in Iraq." -George Bush, October 13th, 2004

"I'm very proud in this race to have the support of General John Shalikashvili, former chairman of the Joint Chiefs of Staff; Admiral William Crowe, former chairman of the Joint Chiefs of Staff; General Tony McPeak, who ran the air war for the president's father and did a brilliant job, supporting me..." -John Kerry, September 30th, 2004

In addition to highlighting their own positive affiliations, the candidates also underscored their opponent's negative affiliations:

"Bush and his friends took [the right to import prescription drugs] out in the House, and now you don't have that right. The president blocked you from the right to have less expensive drugs from Canada." -John Kerry, October 13th, 2004

"The National Journal named Senator Kerry the most liberal Senator of all. And that's saying something in that bunch. You

---

[14] Those familiar with Jimmy Carter's presidency will recall Billy Carter's marketing of Billy Beer as an embarrassment for the President.

might say that took a lot of hard work." -George Bush, October 8th, 2004

    Bush's quote exemplifies one of the main strategies by which Republicans sought to undermined Kerry's credibility—the Bush campaign consistently deployed messages associating Kerry with everything that appeared liberal and elitist. The campaign unceasingly reminded voters that Kerry hails from Massachusetts. They highlighted the fact that Kerry drinks green tea and goes windsurfing. When several key newspapers endorsed Kerry, the Bush camp argued that the support was a direct result of Kerry's association with the liberal media. They attacked his family, and particularly his wife Teresa, for being wealthy and elitist. It can be argued that these often repeated negative associations took their toll and effectively reduced Kerry's credibility in the eyes of middle-class Americans.

Intrinsic credibility

Intrinsic credibility is the credibility that a speaker builds during the persuasive appeal. Similar to extrinsic credibility, intrinsic credibility depends on the persuader's ability to convey: 1) qualification, 2) security, and 3) dynamism. Intrinsic credibility is a key tool in winning the support of an audience that is undecided prior to the persuasive appeal. It is also important in addressing supportive audiences because its absence can erode an audience's confidence in the speaker over time regardless of her level of extrinsic credibility.

    Specific persuasive appeals offer audience members the opportunity to judge the candidate through their own experience of the speaker. As is the case with extrinsic credibility, a persuader needs to analyze his audience and the context before deciding which aspects of their position to highlight during the appeal. In this sense, a persuader must be capable of responding to slight changes in context resulting from recent events, while remaining cognizant of how those events may be understood in terms of a particular audience's motivations. An example of this would be the importance of a persuader's sense of security. As September 11th recedes, the American people may become less fearful and therefore more interested in a candidate's qualification. A good persuader realizes these variables and adapts accordingly.

Qualification

During the persuasive appeal a speaker must be able to demonstrate qualification with general intelligence, clarity of thought, and familiarity with his subject matter. Voters assess such attributes by reading campaign literature, watching debates, or interacting with a canvasser at the door. In general, people evaluate qualification for office by examining the claims made during the appeal. Whether they are consciously aware of it or not, voters ask such questions as: Do the claims make sense both logically and in terms of personal experience? Are the claims believable? Do the solutions offered address the problems at hand?

If a persuader fails to demonstrate qualification during an appeal, the audience often concludes that the speaker lacks legitimacy. This is particularly problematic for political persuaders because voters feel uncomfortable having illegitimate, unqualified people represent them. They rightly conclude that if the persuader is unable to present his ideas clearly and convincingly during a campaign, they cannot effectively represent their constituents while in office. There are exceptions to this type of judgment, however. If the audience members themselves are overwhelmed by the information presented or are uncertain about the issues being debated, they may not judge the persuader harshly on the basis of his qualification.

Security

A speaker conveys security to her audience when she is able to convince them that she is trustworthy and believable. Security, however, is not limited to trust alone, it also refers to a speaker's ability to appear friendly and kind. Typically, the more likable the candidate appears, the more secure the audience feels. A persuader can increase an audience's sense of security by telling relevant stories, using self-deprecating humor, and engaging in non-verbal behaviors such as touch or facial expressions. In essence, a persuader can convey security by subtly assuring the audience "you can trust me because I mean what I say and I'm a lot like you."

Depending on the topic and the context, security can be the most important factor in establishing the speaker's credibility. When audience members are grappling with a high level of uncertainty, they will place greater demands on the speaker to offer them security. During the 2004 election, Americans struggled with uncertainty on many fronts. The economy was in recession, a foreign enemy had attacked the country, and the culture wars were in full swing. As a result, Americans' desire for security was quite high and thus security was a central theme throughout the 2004 campaign season. Republicans, and particularly President Bush, saw this as their strongpoint and continually returned to it. Bush consistently asserted that he could offer Americans greater security because he stood firm and took bold actions. He also successfully convinced a fair number of Americans that Kerry did not offer safety because he was inconsistent. In sum, during a time of great uncertainty, Bush effectively portrayed himself as the safe bet.

Dynamism

Dynamism is the ability of a speaker to gain identification with and admiration from an audience. Research suggests that in general, dynamic figures are seen as bold, frank, and energetic. Such dynamism can be found in various aspects of the appeal from posture and other forms of nonverbal communication to word choice and tone. Dynamism is perhaps the most important characteristic signaling intrinsic credibility in today's fast-paced, visually oriented and emotionally-based culture because it works to quickly gain the audience's attention. This has become especially true in the last decade, when dynamic messages from advertisers are the norm, and audiences have come to expect the same from candidates courting their vote.

Research on dynamism suggests that it is a character trait that cannot be learned. Similar to charisma, it appears to be an innate characteristic found in a small number of speakers. One of the most dynamic speakers in contemporary American culture is former President Bill Clinton. While it is clear that Clinton is a brilliant man, what people find most remarkable about him is his ability to connect with his audience and energize them through his speaking. Take, for example, his performance in the 1992 debate against George H. Bush and Ross Perot. In the 1992 campaign, the Republicans deployed tactics similar to those aimed at Kerry in the 2004 election. They sought to undermine Clinton's credibility by highlighting a pattern of inconsistency. Clinton confronted this directly and dynamically:

"That's what's wrong with Mr. Bush. His whole deal is you've gotta be for it or against it, you can't make it better. I believe we can be better. I think the American people are sick and tired of either/or solutions, people being pushed in the corner, polarized to extremes. I want to think they want somebody with common sense who can do what's best for the American people. And I'd be happy to discuss these other issues, but I can't believe he is accusing me of getting on both sides." -Bill Clinton, October 11th, 1992

Many Democrats cannot believe that a large number of Americans found George Bush to be a more credible candidate for President than John Kerry. They argue that Kerry was clearly the more intelligent candidate and the candidate with stronger moral character. But it serves us well to remember that intelligence is only one factor an audience considers in assessing credibility, and that in public life perception of character matters more than true character. In cases where an audience knows little about the topic themselves, they may tend to discount the importance of qualification because they feel they lack the ability to accurately assess it. In addition, when an audience has a heightened need for security, they may rely on gut instinct and appearances more than in-depth analysis. This is especially true when the audience confronts an overload of conflicting information which audience members do not feel competent to sort through.

It is also important to remember that in highly divisive political races, character is easily called into question. In the 2004 election, Americans were ultimately less concerned with Bush's qualifications than they were comforted by the security he conveyed and motivated by the dynamism he demonstrated. While it seems irrational for voters to select a candidate based on their energy rather than their intelligence, dozens of examples in the last decade demonstrate that this is often the case.

Better Persuasion: 3 Things You Can Do

1) Work to improve the credibility of the Democratic Party

Each person attempting to persuade on behalf of the Democrats is hindered by the Party's reputation for indecision and absence of moral conviction. The Democratic Party has a lot of work to do to regain lost credibility. While this will take some time, each Progressive can do his part to improve the reputation of the Party at the county and state level. Here are a few things you can do:

- Encourage members of the Party to become more visible in the community, particularly by doing community service.
- Form an outreach group that explores and responds to the concerns of faith communities in your area.
- When given an opportunity to speak to somebody about the Party be honest: acknowledge the Party's past problems and highlight ways in which they are being addressed.

2) <u>Build strong</u> associations at the grassroots level through the house party model

House parties are one of the best organizing tools that emerged from the 2004 election. Using the Internet to advertise and coordinate, hosts open their homes to their friends, neighbors, and like-minded strangers. The host of the party often offers refreshments and then introduces the speaker who will talk about a specific political topic, ask for questions, and often solicit donations for the Party or a candidate. This tool is very effective because people are much more likely to believe messages coming from their neighbors than those coming from people they do not know. They are also much more willing to become involved when they realize they will be part of a community when they do so. During the 2004 election, thousands of house parties took place nationwide. Many of the networks established through the parties remain today. Consider hosting a house party in your home or the home of a friend. Use www.meetup.com or www.party2win.com to register your party or to find other parties. The model will only truly serve its purpose if people use it to build alliances prior to elections.

3) Identify and support dynamic candidates

Unfortunately, political consultants waste a lot of time crafting images of candidates that convey intrinsic credibility. We've all heard about the attempts to make presidential candidates Al Gore more exciting, John Kerry more down-to-earth, or Bob Dole more hip. As we know all too well, these attempts do not work, only serving to make the persuader look inauthentic to voters. Unlike most persuasion tools in this book, dynamism cannot be learned. You either have it or you don't. Democrats need to find people who do. Bill Clinton is proof that a candidate can be both dynamic and well-qualified. In selecting candidates, the dynamic qualities of an individual should be assessed upfront. In the mediated age, it is important to recognize that <u>candidates who</u>

appear too wooden or rigid, or even contemplative on complex issues will suffer at the polls. Get involved with your Party and participate in recruiting dynamic people to run for office and lead campaign activities.

CHAPTER 7

THAT WHICH UNITES US...AND DIVIDES US

Identification

As discussed in the previous chapter, a persuader's credibility is linked to the audience's perception of his likeableness. There are several factors that can contribute to a messenger's likeableness, but the most influential is *identification*. In fact, identification is one of the most important aspects of persuasion in general. Human beings always seek points of similarity, or ways in which they can identify with one another. Examples of this include pleasant exchanges about the weather, questions about musical preferences, or other small talk when people are first getting to know each other. It should therefore come as no surprise that audiences find speakers who are similar to them more likeable than those who bear no resemblance. Even one point of commonality will encourage an audience to identify more broadly with the speaker's interests and ideas. As a result, audiences are more likely to accept the claims of persuaders they identify with.

Progressive persuaders can make more effective appeals by emphasizing points of commonality with their fellow Americans. As recent elections have shown, Americans want to be able to relate to their political leaders. Making note of existing similarities is important because when Americans feel they have something in common with a candidate, they are more likely to trust and support that person. Identification is doubly important in political persuasion because voters are asking the candidate to be their voice in the public sphere. While there might not be enough time for the canvasser to firmly establish common ground with the person at the doorstep and the person running for office may, in all truth, actually be quite different from his constituents, such persuaders should still look for and highlight points of identification in their appeals. Identification is communicated in three primary ways: 1) nonverbally, 2) manner of speech, and 3) choice of language.

Nonverbal Identification
It might surprise you to learn that the majority of human communication is nonverbal. In fact, some researchers have suggested that nonverbal cues account for over 80% of communication. In addition, people often attribute more weight to nonverbal messages than verbal ones. One study indicated that the impact of a speaker's performance was determined 55% by nonverbal communication, 38% by voice quality, and only 7% by the words they used (Mehrabian, 1971).

A wide range of nonverbal cues can encourage identification. At a basic level, audiences are more likely to listen to someone of their own race, age, or gender. Political persuaders implicitly recognize this phenomenon when they size up a candidate in relation to the average voter in their district, or seek out particular types of speakers to address certain audiences. They understand, for example, that a young person would generally be a more effective persuader in front of a group of college students than an elderly person would be, specifically because there is a higher level of identification.

At a more abstract level of nonverbal communication, a persuader conveys similarity through clothing and body language. Political candidates demonstrate common ground with the average American by wearing emblems like an American flag or a sports team logo. They also ensure that the public sees them in informal attire, as when George Bush wears jeans to work on his farm or Bill Clinton jogs in sweat pants and a T-shirt. Even more subtly, persuaders build identification by keeping an open and relaxed posture and using familiar gestures like the thumbs-up sign.

A final way in which nonverbal identification is used in politics is found in the many images displayed throughout

110

campaigns. One of the most common images candidates feature in their campaign literature is pictures of themselves with their family and pets. This image portrays an easy similarity. It shows that the candidate has a domestic life with everyday concerns and he values his family in the same way as ordinary Americans do. Other common images include the candidate touring a factory or visiting a school. These images tell the viewer that the candidate is not above the people he wishes to serve, and that he maintains an active interest in their daily lives.

While everyone involved in politics uses nonverbal identification, some do it better than others. In the 2004 election, American voters identified more strongly with George Bush than John Kerry. As a result, the average American found Bush to be more likable and more trustworthy. In explaining this perception, voters often cited Bush's informal approach and "good old boy" persona. This was exemplified by such things as his swagger, Texas accent, and short-sleeved shirts. On the other hand, Kerry's "wooden appearance" and formal manner made it more difficult for him to nonverbally convey common ground. In essence, his nonverbal communication constructed a barrier between him and his audience.

Manner of Speaking
When building identification, how you say something is just as important as what you say. Political persuaders can signal commonality with an audience by speaking in a manner that is comfortable, familiar, and easy to understand. This approach not only allows audience members to comprehend the appeal, but also to feel that the appeal is directed at them. In order to increase a sense of identification, persuaders need to match their manner of speaking to the audience's by considering such aspects as tone, word choice, and types of examples.

When speaking to a broad and diverse audience, as is common in politics, the rule of thumb is to act like you are with people you know, and talk like you are addressing a 6th grade class. Most journalists and television reporters write stories with this in mind, and many Americans have come to expect informality and simplicity in public communication. Even though they know better in principle, many Democrats have ignored this fact. Because they feel much more at home with more formal discourse, these Democrats often forget how this is interpreted by the average American. Compare the two responses to a question regarding government waste during the debate between candidates for the Oklahoma Senate seat in 2004. The first, which is filled with jargon and complex economic relationships, was made by the Democrat. The second, which is much simpler and to the point, was made by the Republican.

"Well, I think there are some straightforward things we can do. First, we have to keep the problem in perspective. As a percentage of our Gross Domestic Product, the budget deficit this year is not what it was in the 1980s and early 1990s. And, of course, we've had some extraordinary events happen in the recent years, but that's not to say we shouldn't get ourselves back on a path toward fiscal solvency. And I release, in my campaign, a detailed plan to do just this. It starts with this. The Government Accounting Office says that we have about $50 billion—$50 billion in various forms of waste, fraud, and abuse that prudent management from the Senate and the House and its oversight could eliminate. There are corporate loopholes that are exploited every day to avoid lawful taxation, that the Government Accounting Office says equal about $250 billion a year. I've also proposed eliminating unnecessary and outdated government agencies, things like the Council on Environmental Quality, the Export-Import Bank, things like this." -Brad Carson, October 3rd, 2004

"Sure you can. First of all, Brad wants to hide the ball. There's only 10 percent of the members of Congress that want to spend more money than Brad does. He authored and co-signed onto bills $440 billion compared to $170 billion for the rest of the entire Oklahoma delegation, including the senators and all the rest of the House members. You can't have it both ways. You can't say, "I want to spend more money, spend more money and spend more money' and then say, 'I want to trim a little $50 billion.' The fact is that the Congress has not been responsible with spending. Everybody in America knows that the government is not efficient. We need to have, first of all, a freeze on any increase in government spending except homeland defense and defense. We need to look at every government program." -Tom Coburn, October 3rd, 2004

Once again, the best example of a candidate successfully creating identification with an audience in this way is found in the 2004 presidential election. George Bush repeatedly portrayed himself as a plainspoken person, while John Kerry often struggled with the fact that his natural tone and word choice did not match that of most Americans. While Democrats assumed the public would reject President Bush because of his missteps in communication, most Americans identified with him for that very reason. They saw him as an everyday person. Bush also demonstrated that he could laugh at himself when he misspoke, thereby solidifying identification through a sense of humility and self-deprecation. As Bush was creating identification, Democrats further distanced themselves from the public by continually making fun of Bush's lack of intelligence. Our mockery of the President provided clear evidence of our intellectual elitism and ultimately demonstrated that we had no interest in identifying with the average American.

Language Choices

A final approach which can intentionally increase an audience's sense of identification with a persuader is through choosing specific language to use throughout the appeal. There are three approaches to creating identification through language.

The first of these rhetorical tools is *explicit identification*. In this approach, the persuader makes specific claims of common ground concerning such things as class, education, and values. Because this can be too obvious if overused, it should only be done a few times in any appeal. A good example of explicit identification can be found in Vice-Presidential candidate Dick Cheney's appeal during his debate with John Edwards:

"I come from relatively modest circumstances. My grandfather never even went to high school. I'm the first in my family to graduate from college. I carried a ticket in the Brotherhood of Electrical Workers for six years. I've been laid off, been hospitalized without health insurance. So I have some ideas of the problems that people encounter" -Dick Cheney, October 5th, 2004

This was a very effective rhetorical move on Cheney's part because, unlike Bush, he lacks identification in other areas and is often associated with the upper class rather than working class Americans.

The second approach, *implicit identification,* is much subtler and can therefore be used more frequently. In this approach, the persuader creates an "assumed we" by using pronouns like *we, our,* and *us,* and phrases like *fellow Americans.* Many political messages are peppered with such examples because the persuader knows they provide an easy way to group together diverse people and subtly identify with an audience who lacks obvious common ground with the persuader. Both candidates used implicit identification during the 2004 presidential debates:

"My fellow Americans, as I've said at the very beginning of this debate, both President Bush and I love this country very much. There's no doubt, I think, about that. But we have a different set of convictions about how we make our country stronger here at home and respected again in the world." -John Kerry, September 30th, 2004

"But again, I repeat to my fellow citizens, the best way to protection is to stay on the offense." -George Bush, September 30th, 2004

A final way political persuaders can use language to build identification is through the *creation of a common enemy.* In this case, the speaker creates identification by referencing an enemy that both she and the audience can oppose as a unified front. In making the argument for Iraq War, President Bush constructed

Saddam Hussein as a common enemy in the eyes of those in power and in turn, the eyes of the American people:

"Members of the Congress of both political parties and members of the United Nations Security Council agree that Saddam Hussein is a threat to peace and must disarm. We agree that the Iraqi dictator must not be allowed to threaten America and the world with horrible poisons and diseases and gases and atomic weapons. Since we all agree on this goal, the issue is: how can we best achieve it?" -George Bush, October 7th, 2002.

Democrats have also used this tool, not only to suggest common enemies in terms of foreign affairs, but also on domestic issues. In the Vice-Presidential debate, John Edwards sought to build identification through the common enemy of insurance companies:

"John Kerry and I are always going to stand with the Valerie Lakeys of the world, and not with the insurance companies."
-John Edwards, October 5th, 2004

All three of the strategies discussed above aid the persuader in small ways to demonstrate identification during specific persuasive appeals. But it is important to recognize that such rhetorical moves will never substitute for the identification candidates need to build over the long term. Progressives must take a two-pronged approach. They need to do a better job at broadening their potential audience by keying on commonly held values and priorities that resonate with many Americans, at the same time they target constituencies who share a Progressive vision and are likely to go to the polls. In order to be successful in building identification, we need to do deep audience analysis to better understand what core values and key issues Americans hold in common at this time.

We also need to focus our attention on audiences who consistently vote. One of the hard lessons coming out of the 2004 election was that young Americans are among the least likely to vote. Despite all the efforts by organizations like The Young Voter Project and America Comes Together (ACT) there was little reversal in this clear trend. As we approach future elections, we need to shift our attention and our resources to other constituencies. In the end, while Bush may have picked up a few swing votes with his use of short-term identification, he won the election because of his ability to demonstrate true common ground with conservative Christians and fearful patriots. Democrats need to articulate their causes, find their voice, and then build identification through authentic points of commonality.

Division

The use of a common enemy to demonstrate similarity lays bare the other side of identification—division. In some respects, division is a natural by-product of identification, because creating an *us* necessitates a *them.* Division is part of the human condition whereby we recognize ourselves as separate from others. While philosophers ponder this, persuaders use it to their advantage. In the same vein good persuaders use credibility, division is used in conjunction with identification as the persuader emphasizes both her similarity to the audience and her opponent's dissimilarity.

Political persuaders typically use division to convince their audience to join them in the fight against a specific enemy. In politics, this is most often constructed along the lines of our national identity. Historically, American identity has been built primarily around a narrative that has America saving the world from the evil other. Many of our political programs and policies depend on the rhetorical construction of a division between good and evil. For instance, most of the persuasive appeals concerning the military are founded on the assumption that America's way of life is threatened by other ideologies and other people who are not like us. Division is also used on the domestic front. Examples include dividing Americans along racial and class lines, pitting urban concerns against rural ones, and relegating dissidents to the margins of society by effectively pointing out that they are not like average Americans.

For those wishing to effectively apply the language of division, it is important to realize that its use can be quite complex. While human beings accept some level of division, they are uncomfortable with the uncertainty it creates. Political persuaders must choose appropriate enemies by closely examining the context. As suggested earlier, the 2004 election, which took place in the midst of war and economic uncertainty, presented a context where American citizens needed to feel unified even when it was difficult to ignore great division. In that context, the only acceptable division was the division between America and the terrorists. Signs of this desire abounded: *United We Stand* ribbons appeared on cars, and all forms of dissent were discouraged. The context was embodied in Bush's statement "You're either with us or with the terrorists."

The Republicans understood the context in which the 2004 election took place largely because they worked to create it. They realized that a feeling of unity offered Americans a greater sense of security and assured them that the country was on the right track. As a result, Republicans chose to act as if the country was united. The only internal division Bush and other Republican candidates acknowledged was the division between Kerry and key players in the Iraq War: the military, coalition allies, and Iraqis. Bush created this division in the first debate:

"I don't see how you can lead this country to succeed in Iraq if you say wrong war, wrong time, wrong place. What message does that send our troops? What message does that send our allies? What message does that send the Iraqis?… I don't appreciate when a candidate for president denigrates the contribution of these brave soldiers," -George Bush, September 30th, 2004

Kerry and other Democratic candidates also used division. However, while Democratic and Republican rhetoric about external enemies was similar, Democrats also emphasized internal divisions. This strategy included dividing the American public from President Bush, dividing the average American from the very wealthy American, and dividing people culturally. While this approach was very effective for rallying committed Progressives, it was not persuasive to the wider American public. The desire for unity made it unlikely that the average American would accept much less respond to, strong suggestions of internal division.

With lessons from the 2004 election in mind, Democrats need to mold their message with a keen eye towards the current context. There is some sense that as the context changes, with events like Hurricane Katrina shining light on the lack of infrastructure at home and public opinion souring on the Iraq War, that dividing Americans from President Bush may be more effective. At the same time, we can build better identification with a broader number of Americans by consistently demonstrating that the Bush Administration and Republicans in general are deceiving the American people for their own profit and the benefit of the hyper-wealthy. The corruption scandals around politicians like Tom DeLay and lobbyists like Jack Abramhoff provide a great backdrop for these appeals.

Better Persuasion: 3 Things You Can Do

1) Find out more about your fellow Americans.

Progressives should learn more about their fellow Americans. Viewing Republican voters in the so-called "Red" states as stupid, brainwashed, or hypocritical is both narrow-minded and ineffective. Our tendency to cast tens of millions of Americans in this light costs us much more than it gains. How can we persuade these people if we are proud of the fact that we are nothing like them? We need to take Red America seriously and find out more about their motivations. After all, many of them use to vote for Democrats and many of them feel the economic squeeze from decades of Republican policies. All Progressives living in Blue counties need to look beyond their borders. We can't afford to believe that our way of thinking is pervasive. Every election reminds us that it is not. To find out more about how your fellow Americans think you should:

- Read Thomas Frank's *What's the Matter with Kansas.*
- Visit the webpage of a more conservative paper in your state once a week. Note the issues covered and read the Letters to the Editor section.
- Attend civic meetings, church, or public hearings in the suburbs.

2) Find out more about the Democratic Party.

There is no doubt that the Democratic Party needs to reflect on who they are and what they stand for. They also need to strive for consistency and discipline in their messages. But each Progressive also needs to spend time learning about what Democrats have been fighting for. Because the Republicans have been so much louder and clearer with their agenda, many Americans do not feel that Democratic policies are truly in their interest. If each of us was better able to articulate the key policies of our Party with two or three strong examples, we could clearly demonstrate commonalities between the Party and the people we are trying to persuade. Each Progressive can take these 4 easy steps:

1. Find the Party platform on the Internet and read it. Print it out and make copies.
2. Once you are able to articulate a few of the Party's positions and policies, think of a specific person in your life who reluctantly voted Republican during the last election.
3. Find 3 points of commonality between the Party and that person, and build a persuasive appeal to that person using those points.
4. Try the appeal on that person and see how they respond.

3) Focus on division in terms of class, if the context allows.

If there is one thing the Republicans do not want Democrats to talk about, it's class. Republicans have been very successful in constructing an alternative division based on culture. A commitment to uniting Americans based on their economic class must be at the heart of the Democrats' reemergence. This unification will partly be built through the highlighting of the division between ordinary Americans and the very wealthy. Using language focusing on character and not on economic success, Democrats need to point out that the very wealthy do not care about average Americans. We need to make the point, consistently and repeatedly, that a small percentage of Americans has used the labor of other people to insulate themselves against any misfortune. The very rich manipulate our public policy to ensure the continuance of their privileged existence. Statistics can help you in creating this division:

- There is less upward mobility now than there was 20 years ago.
- Many members of Bush's pro-war administration avoided military service themselves including Bush himself, Dick Cheney, Richard Perle, and Paul Wolfowitz.
- In 2004, the number of millionaires rose at the same time the poverty level in the US increased for the 4th straight year in a row.

In addition to focusing on the hyper-wealthy, Progressives should also highlight the division between corporations and American citizens. While it has been slow going, many Americans are beginning to see how many perks and privileges corporations get from our government. As corporations are nameless, faceless entities, it is easier for them to be vilified. Our appeals should consistently point out striking inequities between citizens and corporations in terms of tax burden. For example, some Progressives in the Portland, OR area made bumper stickers that say, *I pay more taxes than PGE-Enron* highlighting the fact that most corporations in the state pay roughly $10 a year in corporate taxes.

CHAPTER 8

WORDS THAT MATTER

Experience teaches us that certain words can be extraordinarily powerful. For example, when Americans hear the word *traitor* they feel a range of negative emotions including intense anger or betrayal. When they hear the phrase *land of the brave*, they feel a very different set of emotions such as pride and hope. Such strong feelings often lead to swift judgment such as "the traitor must be punished" or "we must protect our homeland." These judgments may cause an audience to act without discussion or condone the actions of others using such terms without question or objection. This is particularly the case when the terms are ambiguous and the audience addressed has little direct experience with the topic being discussed.

Much of our language is rife with ambiguity. Our use of many common terms assumes a consensus on their meaning that simply does not exist. Take, for example, the term *evil*. Though many persuaders regularly use the term to provoke emotion, pass judgment, and justify solutions, very few people would agree on exactly what *evil* is or what actions can be classified specifically as *evil*. In fact, many people would say, "it depends." And it does. It depends on many things such as the perspective of the audience and the motives of the person under consideration. But often, when we hear certain terms, we assume general agreement on their meaning and are therefore unlikely to ask clarifying questions.

Political persuaders use the ambiguity of language to their advantage. They understand that contemporary culture demands that messages be conveyed quickly, simply, and often dramatically in order to capture an audience's attention and make their point.

Language devices are essential in such a climate as they allow persuaders to encapsulate many different meanings into a handful of simple terms. In addition, language devices often lend intensity to messages, particularly when words are used to create vivid imagery for an audience. Such imagery allows the audience to better picture themselves in relationship to the topic being discussed, thereby building greater identification and interest in the message. Political persuaders recognize that language devices improve a message's effectiveness on many levels from the speed of its transmission, to the number of people likely to respond, to the strength of their response.

Persuaders can use a whole range of language devices (i.e. repetition, alliteration, antithesis, personification, etc.). A few key devices are explored in greater detail below.

<u>Metaphor</u>

Metaphor is one of the most common language devices found in political persuasion. It employs the comparison of two things that may not be overtly similar in order to lend the feelings and experiences associated with one object to another object. While metaphor has historically been regarded as a means of adding flourish to language, it has more recently been seen as an integral means to understand the world we live in. This is because metaphors permeate not only our communication, but also our way of thinking. They help us to see abstract principles in more concrete and more familiar ways. They also expand the potential of language to better represent the complexity or richness of human experience. Lakoff and Johnson (1980) suggest that metaphors work towards a variety of ends in language. They:

Direct attention to particular concepts and relationships
The metaphors of a culture can act like frames, selecting and making salient certain aspects of a larger reality. As such, the types of metaphor used in a culture can signal that culture's priorities or what it wishes to emphasize in interpretation. In the

123

United States we often rely on economic metaphors such as *put a lot of stock in him* or *weigh the costs and benefits of that decision.*

Hide the uncomfortable or controversial
Metaphors can be used to disguise points of difference or discomfort. A person might use metaphors to rhetorically hide those things his audience may disagree with or those things the audience may not wish to be confronted with directly. An example of this can be found in the language of the military when they use the term *collateral damage* in referring to civilian deaths. The use of such a metaphor allows the speaker to more easily advance their overarching message without hesitation or opposition on the part of the audience.

Create new perspectives
Metaphors can introduce new possibilities or avenues of thought, effectively extending how we conceptualize and characterize the world around us. Changing the metaphors one uses can change the way a person thinks. For example, relating life to a game will naturally produce a different perspective than seeing life as a journey.

Direct behavior
The way in which we talk about something may not only impact our perspective, but also lead us to act in certain ways. Because metaphors can affect the way we conceptualize the world, they can also impact the way we act and react to it. For example, people who understand education to be a tool useful in gaining employment may very well choose different classes than people who see education as an awakening. In such a case, the individual's behavior emerges from her perspective.

Humans use metaphors to such an extent that many such terms are no longer seen as metaphors. Some well known examples include: *grab the bull by the horns, throw some light on the subject,* and *feeling blue.* While metaphors can be used purely for aesthetic purposes, persuaders tend to use these devices to increase the likelihood that an audience will react favorably to their messages. By drawing a connection between something the audience already knows and a new or more abstract concept, the persuader offers both common ground and a different perspective.

In addition, metaphors that are widely recognized by general audiences can be used to support arguments. Archetypal metaphors, common across cultures and typically rooted in nature, are often found in persuasion. For instance, when we hear that America has *weathered a storm* or that we are *battling dark forces*, we are encouraged to support policies based on our assumptions concerning storms and darkness.

Metaphors are especially useful in political persuasion where an audience may not have direct experience with the topic or be wary of certain actions if they were discussed frankly. Metaphors are also used in political rhetoric to create a feeling of shared knowledge, thereby building identification between the speaker and her audience, as well as between audience members. It is the efficiency of metaphor which allows for effective identification. For example, Kazin suggests that the term *middle America* used in political language since the 1970s "evoked simultaneously, three compelling meanings; the unstylish, traditional expanse that lay between the two coasts; an egalitarian social status most citizens either claimed or desired; and a widespread feeling of being squeezed between penthouse and ghetto—between a condescending elite above and scruffy demonstrators and welfare recipients below" (1995, p. 253).

Metaphors are abundant in political rhetoric and the contemporary picture is no exception. Not only have metaphors been used to classify particular target audiences like *soccer moms*, *security moms*, and *NASCAR dads*, they have been used to describe different political policies. Because these metaphors help us to understand what is at stake and what action should be taken, they serve as a powerful component of our decision-making. The clearest contemporary example of how metaphors impact the public's perception of a policy can be found in the Administration's use of the *War on Terror.*

The *War on Terror*[15]

After our country was attacked on September 11th, the Bush Administration was faced with a complex problem. On the one hand, they recognized that our attackers were not like any enemy we had previously faced and that our response would have to be unique. On the other, they understood that in order to gain support from the American public for that response, they would have to package it in familiar terms. As a result, the Administration and the media quickly began to use the term *War on Terror.* This phrase is metaphoric, as it tries to relate our response to terrorism to that of previously understood military endeavors.

While the packaging of our response to September 11th was necessary, it came with an expensive price tag. Because the Administration used the language of war, we quickly began acting like we were engaging in a typical war. As a result, Americans had certain expectations they brought to the term and to the specific conflicts within the war on terror, namely the Iraq War. First, they expected that there was a definable enemy that could be defeated. This is evidenced by Tony Blair's claim on November 20th, 2003 which suggests that we could "rid our world of this evil once and for all" and Vice President Cheney's statements that "Our strategy in the war on terror is based on a clear understanding of the enemy and a clear assessment of our national interest" -Dick Cheney July 24th, 2003. Used in this way, the metaphor ignores the reality that fighting terrorists is different than fighting a war against a particular nation. Over time, the more military activity we engage in the Middle East, the more terrorists we will create. As our military endeavors impact the lives of everyday citizens in the Middle East, we fulfill the roles

---

[15] <http://webserve.govst.edu/pa/>

Islamic radicals have crafted for us. We quickly become invaders and infidels.

Second, the American public expected that there would be a clear timeline with a definitive exit strategy. We now know that this is unlikely as various people within the Administration and the military suggest that it could take a decade or more. Many voices have been calling for the type of exit strategy typically associated with war. When they are told that such a strategy, or even a basic timeline regarding US strategy in the region, cannot be given under the circumstances, they quickly find that the metaphor of war does not hold up.

Finally, in line with expectations regarding an exit strategy, many Americans believed that there would be a clear victory. This victory was originally believed to come in the form of a quick invasion warmly welcomed by the Iraqi people. Later it became tied to the returning of power to a suitably trained Iraqi military and the establishment of a viable constitution. None of these things have come to pass. And yet, because we see ourselves as fighting a war, we cannot leave the region. Leaving at this juncture would signal defeat. As a result, more and more Americans and Iraqis are losing their lives. In truth, most of us know that there will be no clear victory in the War on Terror.

The metaphor *War on Terror* demonstrates just how powerful language terms can be in constructing behavior and setting expectations. If the Administration had chosen less familiar but more accurate language, we might be on a very different path at this time. Because the Administration chose to equate our response to September 11th with war, we are at war today with no clear end in sight.

God & Devil Terms

In every culture there are rhetorically loaded terms that automatically evoke either positive or negative emotions. These are classified as *God & Devil* terms.[16] Upon hearing a *God term*, the

---

[16] Richard Weaver, 1953

listener has a strong reaction of positive feelings. When they hear a *Devil term* they have the same type of reaction with negative feelings. Examples of God terms include *democracy, community,* and *progress.* Examples of Devil terms include *fascist, racist,* and *greed.* Such terms are quite similar to, but often broader than *ideographs,* which will be discussed in the following chapter. Like all language devices, God and Devil terms depend on both audience perception and the cultural/political context. The power of these terms can change with time and circumstance. In addition, one audience's God term can be another audience's Devil term. Such is the case with the term *environmentalist:* most Progressives respond positively to this term, while most Conservatives respond negatively.

Not surprisingly, political persuaders use God terms to build positive associations with themselves and their message. Persuaders also hope to create an atmosphere where questioning them or their propositions is frowned upon, equating such inquiries as an assault on the goodness inherent in the God terms themselves. This is readily apparent in the title of the Patriot Act which is rhetorically designed to prohibit analysis or opposition. In a similar vein, persuaders use Devil terms to build negative associations with their opponents. They rely on the ambiguity of the terms in combination with the audience's powerful emotional response to elicit agreement.

In the contemporary political picture, it is easy to identify several key God and Devil terms. Two God terms frequently found in this past election season were *small businesses* and *our troops.* Political persuaders on both sides used these terms to elicit positive responses to policy choices or proposals. They also assumed that the audience's immediate positive reaction would protect the policies themselves from intense scrutiny. The following are a few examples of how each term can be deployed:

Our troops
"Now, that's not a good way to build support and reduce the risk for *our troops* and make America safer. I'm going to get the

training done for *our troops*. I'm going to get the training of the Iraqis done faster. And I'm going to get our allies back to the table." -John Kerry, September 30th, 2004

"Like you, I'm concerned with the deficit. But I'm not going to shortchange *our troops* in harm's way." -George Bush, October 8th, 2004

In the previous examples, *our troops* is used as a God term to demonstrate everything from Bush's moral character to Kerry's foreign policy plans. Most notably, the troops are frequently presented as being in constant danger. Constructing the appeal in this way justifies a wide variety of actions including large deficit spending. After all, who would object to spending money to protect *our troops*?

The power of this term can also be seen in the way critics of specific policies regarding the war must preface any questions or critique with overt statements of support. For example, a leading member of the Congressional Black Caucus delivered the following statement before taking issue with the Administration and the Iraq War:

"We support our troops with everything we have got. As I often say, we support *our troops* 1 million percent, but the fact is that, if justice is to prevail, if peace is to really come to this world, we also need to know and the American citizens need to know whether those troops, while we applaud them over and over again, whether they are receiving justice when they ask the question in the letters to the congressman and their representatives and to their Senators asking what do we have to do to get the things we need to address this war we are in? So I want to make it very clear that there is not the slightest bit of reluctance to support *our troops*. We do. But now we must begin to answer some questions, we presented these questions to the President before, and we will present them over and over again." -Elijah Cumings, Oct. 8th, 2003

Small business

"In addition to that, we're going to allow people 55 to 64 to buy into Medicare early. And most importantly, we give *small businesses* a 50 percent tax credit so that after we lower the cost of health care, they also get, whether they are self-employed or a *small business*, a lower cost to be able to cover their employees." -John Kerry, October 13th, 2004

"I believe the best way to help our *small businesses* is not only through small-business loans, which we have increased since I've been the president of the United States, but to unbundle government contracts." -George Bush, October 13th, 2004

"Working with Jim Bunning and others in Congress, President Bush has taken strong, confident steps to get the economy growing again. The President signed into law three separate tax relief measures, resulting in significant tax relief for millions of American families and *small businesses*." -Dick Cheney, March 12th, 2004

    Small business is used in the following examples not only to enhance the audience's positive response to very different economic proposals, but also to enhance the speaker's own credibility. Because *small business* acts as a God term, political persuaders often use its ambiguity to offer a broad definition so that taxes or regulations on a wide variety of businesses are portrayed negatively. They also tie the term to other powerful persuasive tools like the mythology of the American dream.

    In addition to hearing several God terms throughout the election, the American people also encountered the many Devil terms persuaders included in their appeals. These were used to elicit a quick and negative response encouraging listeners to reject specific people and policies outright, without any deeper analysis. Some of the most commonly used Devil terms by the

Republicans were *liberal* and *trial lawyers.* Several examples of these terms are laid out below.

Liberal

"Only a *liberal* Senator from Massachusetts would say a 49% increase in funding for education was not enough" -George Bush, October 13th, 2004

Kerry.

"The National Journal named Senator ~~Kennedy~~ the most *liberal* senator of all. And that's saying something in that bunch. You might say that took a lot of hard work. The reason I bring that up is that he's proposed $2.2 trillion dollars in new spending…. They don't name him the most *liberal* in the United States Senate because he hasn't shown up to many meetings. They named him that because of his votes. And it's reality. It's just not credible to say he's going to keep taxes down and balance budgets." -George Bush, October 8th, 2004

Republicans made *liberal* a Devil term through consistent rhetorical association of that term with a lack of discipline. They have suggested over and over again that liberals not only lack economic control in spending other people's money, they also lack a moral compass by which to accurately chart the nation's course. This continual association has clearly paid off for the Republicans as most audiences immediately dismiss a policy that is termed *liberal.* More recently, Republicans have focused on one of the Democratic Party's largest financial contributors, making *trial lawyers* a Devil term.

Trial lawyers

"It is stuck in the Senate, because the *trial lawyers* won't act on it. And he put a trial lawyer on the ticket." -George Bush, October 8th, 2004

"Another reason health care costs too much is our abused medical liability system. The culprits are the personal injury *trial lawyers.* And we oppose those predators. We must stop them from

131

twisting American medicine into a litigation lottery where they hit the jackpot and every patient ends up paying." -Bill Frist, August 31st, 2004

Trial lawyer is an example of a term that was intentionally created and deployed to elicit negative feelings despite little clarity about what the term meant. The term has been consistently associated with greed and manipulation so that the average American has an immediate negative reaction when they hear it. As a result of this quick emotional response, they rarely take the time to further investigate the complexity of the topic. In fact, most Americans remain largely unaware that trial lawyers often act on behalf of average Americans like themselves.

Buzzwords

Buzzwords are over-used words or phrases typically found in business or political environments. While some people suggest that these terms simplify communication, particularly in the realm of technology, others have argued that buzzwords are intentionally ambiguous, often being used to impress and/or obscure. The term *buzzwords* emerged in the last decade as the number of such words began to rapidly expand. Buzzwords do not necessarily create the positive or negative reactions associated with God and Devil terms. Instead, the words themselves may sound complex or lofty so audience members are impressed by them. They may also lack any accepted definition so they are difficult to object to. Buzzwords differ from God and Devil terms in another important way – the ambiguity of these terms rarely stimulates a strong emotional reaction. Instead, buzzwords confuse people to the point that they do not act, acquiescing because it is difficult to oppose that which is unclear.

Persuaders often use buzzwords to simplify their language while decreasing the likelihood that they will be challenged on specific policies or perspectives. Unfortunately, many persuaders hide their true intentions in such language devices hoping that the vagueness of the terminology will lead to general acceptance of the message without analysis of the policy itself. In essence, a person is dissuaded from further analysis because of the impenetrable nature of the terms they are confronted with. Political persuaders from both parties and across the board have used buzzwords frequently in the last few years. While many were just space fillers or "empty rhetoric," some were used to obscure, and in some cases excuse, important policy decisions. Below is an analysis of a key buzzword used by the Bush Administration—*Weapons of Mass Destruction:*

WMDs/Weapons of Mass Destruction
"But make no mistake—as I said earlier—we have high confidence that they have *weapons of mass destruction*. That is what this war was about and is about." -Ari Fleischer, April 23rd, 2003

"There is no doubt that the regime of Saddam Hussein possesses *weapons of mass destruction*. And…as this operation continues, those weapons will be identified…" -General Tommy Franks, March 22nd, 2003

"One of our top objectives is to find and destroy the *WMDs*. There are a number of sites." -Patricia Clark, March 22nd, 2003

The term *WMDs* or *Weapons of Mass Destruction* sounds both ambiguous and complex. It also has a military ring to it, relating it to a realm that is typically technical and unfamiliar to most Americans. In addition, the media did not try to define the term for the American people. They never gave it any specificity. Because the term was left largely unexplored and was used almost exclusively in relation to Iraq, political persuaders were able to mask the fact that many countries had similar weapons. The use of this key buzzword disempowered Americans, discouraging them from further analysis and critique. Deploying this term effectively reduced discussion about why America would

133

prioritize a war with Iraq and silenced critics who noted that the US has the largest arsenal of weapons in the world.

Doublespeak

Doublespeak is often found in the language of corporate, military, and political institutions. It is created with the intention of disguising or distorting the true meaning of a policy or activity. The concept comes from George Orwell's *1984*, though Orwell does not use that specific term himself. William Lutz (1989) suggests that doublespeak is "language that pretends to communicate but really doesn't: language that makes the bad seem good, the negative appear positive, the unpleasant appear attractive or at least tolerable" (p. 1). Some examples of doublespeak include *downsizing* for firing, *capital punishment* for the death penalty, and *neutralize, pacify, or expire* for killing.

Doublespeak is a stark example of the power of language, particularly in politics. If an audience has no direct experience with a policy, or no time to read the fine print of a piece of legislation, or no ability to assess the long-term impact of a particular plan, they will respond to the plan based almost solely on the terms it is named by. Political persuaders use doublespeak to gain adherence to things, which the public may rightfully reject if they had all the information. In many ways, the use of doublespeak is cynical politics at its worst. It relies on an under-informed audience who is too tired or too distracted by the pressures of their own lives to discover what the policy is really about. Persuaders who consistently utilize doublespeak spend a lot of time thinking of effective words, and little time thinking of how the suspect policy will negatively affect the Americans they are peddling it to. Unfortunately, there is a growing group of people in politics who are being paid to do just that.

The use of doublespeak is on the rise and it can be found in several places throughout Bush's first term and his campaign for re-election in 2004. Two key environmental policies that depended on simplified and obscured language were the Clear

134

 Skies Act and the Healthy Forest Initiative. These policies were unlikely to gain support from the American public, which remains in favor of strong environmental regulation. As a result, the Administration decided that the most effective approach to presenting the policies was to name the legislation with positive terms. They correctly reasoned that such labels were likely to encourage the average American to support the policies on their face, without further analysis.

Clear Skies Act

The Clear Skies Act, proposed in 2003, seeks to address air quality issues through an expansion of the cap and trade programs whereby one corporation can trade their allowable level of pollution with another. In effect, many analysts have suggested that the Act permits greater industrial air pollution. But Most Americans will probably never know the actual environmental impact of the policy. They assume when they hear the terms associated with the Act that it is legislation designed to reduce pollution thereby creating *clear skies.* And often the Administration encourages that assumption. If, in the future, a person hears that the legislation may actually do the opposite, they are likely to discount that information rather than investigate it, especially when the details of the policy are complex.

Healthy Forest Initiative

The Healthy Forest Initiative was primarily crafted to allow private logging operations greater access to federally owned forests such as those in national parks. This increased access translates into an obvious increase in logging which is loosely justified by the argument that clearing fire prone areas of this land will lead to *healthy forests.* While this is one way to describe *health,* others might rightly argue that a forest, which is persistently logged, particularly using methods like clear cutting, is much less healthy than it was prior to the passage of the Initiative. Of course, as the Administration hoped when it named the policy, the public remains largely unaware of this debate, assuming the Initiative is positive because the term *healthy* has that connotation.

In essence, Bush uses doublespeak to lead his audience to false conclusions concerning these two policies. In his State of the Union Address he says:

"I have sent you Clear Skies legislation that mandates a 79 percent cut in air pollution from power plants over the next 15 years. I have sent you a Healthy Forest initiative to help prevent the catastrophic fires that devastate communities, kill wildlife and burn away millions of acres of treasured forest." -George Bush, January 29th, 2003

In these statements, Bush pairs doublespeak with partial and ambiguous evidence to gain adherence from a public that assumes the policies are good based solely on how they are named.

Better Persuasion: 3 Things You Can Do

1) Discover, develop, and utilize metaphors around the common good or community.

A few rules regarding the use of metaphor:
- In any persuasive appeal, it is better to use one metaphor which the persuader can build on throughout the appeal rather than several metaphors which could create confusion.
- The metaphor itself should be simple and clear. Unlike other forms of persuasion the more ambiguous a metaphor is, the less powerful it will be.
- Metaphors that resonate widely like archetypal metaphors or those that have been frequently used in our culture are more likely to be effective.
- The metaphor should be adaptable so that as context changes the audience can still make the connection.

2) Focus on disrupting Devil terms around taxation.

In the case of Devil terms, we need to challenge those that hurt us by demanding definitions when the Republicans employ them. One interesting idea would be to challenge the demonizing of taxes by running a large-scale ad campaign in major markets demonstrating the many necessary aspects of public life taxes are used for. While this would have to be launched at a national level, every Progressive persuader can incorporate some of that language in her appeals. For example:

- "Nobody likes to pay taxes, but we recognize that it is the price decent people pay for a civilized society."
- "Taxes are important. They are used to make our water safe for drinking, educate our children, and to make sure the elderly and sick don't end up on the street."

3) Continue to focus on the irony of the Republicans' doublespeak.

It will take time and creativity to uncover the hypocrisy and cynicism in such language, but it is an important part of the larger message that Republicans are misleading the country. Every Progressive can select a policy that is wrapped in doublespeak and continually talk about what that policy actually does. Ask people where their positive assumptions come from and challenge the relationship between the name and its actual outcomes. In addition to the Clear Skies Act and Healthy Forest Initiative you can key on:

- No Child Left Behind
- Operation Iraqi Freedom

CHAPTER 9

OUR POLITICAL VOCABULARY

Every society operates based upon a set of generally accepted rules that direct the behavior of its members, suggest appropriate priorities, and reduce the potential for conflict. Politically, that set of rules is referred to as an ideology. Persuasion is the primary goal of ideology because an ideology is ultimately *is* designed and disseminated to keep members of the society in line.

Ideology as persuasion can take many forms, but one of the simplest and most effective is the use of key terms which function as the ideology's vocabulary. These terms embody and signal the political commitments of a culture. As persuaders repeatedly use them throughout society, the terms reinforce those commitments, working seamlessly to encourage specific values and behaviors. Michael McGee[17] (1980) labeled such terms *ideographs.* According to his characterization, an ideograph is:

1) found in political discourse
2) highly abstract, making it difficult for people to agree on its meaning
3) used to justify power and/or excuse behaviors that may typically be seen in a negative light
4) encouraging of conformity by directing behaviors
5) culturally dependent, though similar terms might be deployed by different cultures in different ways
6) implicitly recognized by members of the society. Those who do not respond appropriately are punished

---

[17] http://www.tandf.co.uk/journals/titles/00335630.asp

Like other language devices, ideographs derive much of their power from their ambiguity. They also mirror these devices in their dependence on audience and context, because ideographs can gain and lose prominence in light of who is being addressed and what is currently happening within the political landscape. Ideographs are unique, however, in their wholly political nature and their unmatched ability to get people to respond emotionally and act without thinking. In many ways ideographs are the ultimate God & Devil terms.

Because of the power of such terms, ideographs are often utilized when a persuader is requesting action that entails great cost or contradicts general beliefs held by the audience. In this vein, American political leaders often rely on ideographs to justify controversial policies such as war, imprisonment without charge, and the restriction of personal freedoms.

In the 2004 election, both sides used a number of these terms, but three specific terms surfaced time and time again. One of these ideographs, *freedom,* has been part of our political vocabulary for a long time while the other two, *September 11th* and *terrorist/terrorism,* are quite new. Even though both Democrats and Republicans utilized these words as they campaigned, the fact that Republicans led the response to the attacks on September 11th gave them greater claim to these powerful terms.

Freedom

The power of the term *freedom* is best exemplified by asking two simple questions: How would you react to someone who was planning to take your freedom away? How would you react to someone who said they would protect that freedom? As your response almost certainly demonstrates, we have been socialized to see freedom as intrinsically good and those who wish to take our freedom away as intrinsically evil. In addition, we greatly value those who defend and protect our freedom. Because *freedom* is fundamental to American identity and rooted in the founding of our nation, it should come as no surprise that it is one of our oldest and most effective political terms. What may be more surprising is that freedom is also one of the most ambiguous terms in our culture today. If 100 Americans were asked what freedom was, there would surely be 100 different answers. To some, it would be the ability to live without fear of physical harm, to others it would be a type of responsibility, and to others it would be the opportunity to make various choices. In truth, there is no consensus among Americans as to what *freedom* means.

And yet, political persuaders use the term as if there is a consensus because it offers a sense of unity and provokes a desire for action. The term holds such power because it is central to the identity of the nation and therefore the identity of each American. As Rudy Giuliani said in opening remarks to the United Nations General Assembly Special Session on Terrorism:

"We are defined as Americans by our beliefs—not by our ethnic origins, our race or our religion. Our beliefs in religious freedom, political freedom, and economic freedom—that's what makes an American." -October 1st, 2001

Freedom is also what Americans are most willing to fight and die for. The principle has been at the heart of political persuasion every time our leaders have taken us to war. It is used to explain the necessity of our endeavors and give meaning to the many sacrifices our soldiers are asked to make. The power of the term is evident in the phrase "Freedom Is Not Free." This phrase echoes the history of America and encourages us to believe that our soldiers always fight and die for noble ends.

Political persuaders continue to tie war to the pursuit of freedom in the contemporary context. Not only did the Bush Administration title our initial military intervention in Iraq *Operation Iraqi Freedom*, Republicans used the term in reference to our activities in the Middle East throughout the 2004 election. President Bush used the term in all three of the debates:

"We're pursuing a strategy of *freedom* around the world, because I understand free nations will reject terror. Free nations will answer the hopes and aspirations of their people. Free nations will help us achieve the peace we all want." -George Bush, September 30th, 2004

"Our long-term security depends on our deep faith in liberty. I will continue to promote *freedom* around the world. *Freedom* is on the march. Tomorrow, Afghanistan will be voting for a president. In Iraq, we'll be having free elections, and a free society will make this world more peaceful." -George Bush, October 8th, 2004

"As a result of securing ourselves and routing the Taliban out of Afghanistan, the Afghan people had elections this weekend. And the first voter was a 19-year-old woman. Think about that. *Freedom* is on the march." -George Bush, October 13th, 2004

At the Republican National Convention, New York Governor George Pataki also echoed the connection between *freedom* and our military actions in the Middle East:

"America did not choose this war. But we have a president who chooses to win it. This is no ordinary time. The stakes could not be higher. Fate has handed our generation a grave threat to *freedom*. And fortune has given us a leader who will defend that *freedom*." -George Pataki, September 2nd, 2004

The rhetorical reliance on *freedom* became even more pronounced when no weapons of mass destruction were discovered in Iraq. The term was particularly used to *justify the use of power and/or excuse behaviors that may typically be seen in a negative light*. Republicans defend the war by portraying it as a means to protect our freedom from attack and promote freedom in the Middle East. They also deployed the term to ensure that any vocal opposition would be effectively quelled by equating dissent with the rejection of freedom.

Our Political Vocabulary

<u>September 11th</u>

September 11th is a much newer ideograph. Unlike *freedom*, which has been with us since the founding of our country, *September 11th* became an ideograph several years ago as a result of the attacks on that infamous day. This political term provokes a wide range of emotions, many of which are negative, but some of which are positive. When most people hear the term *September 11th* they remember the tragedy that befell our nation, the innocence of the people who died that day, and the honor of those who died trying to save them. They also feel anger at the people who attacked our country and pride in the fact that the country banded together to help those directly affected by the attacks and heal the nation. In addition, *September 11th* evokes feelings of patriotism and lingering fears about potential attacks from other foreign enemies.

With so many emotions tied to one phrase and the recent nature of the event making them even stronger, political persuaders recognized the value of the term during the 2004 election and beyond. For the last several years, Republicans in particular have used its power to advance a whole host of political positions and activities. They reasoned that if the average American could not be convinced to support war on the basis of anger, perhaps they could be persuaded not to divide the country with dissent or dishonor fellow Americans who responded so bravely on that day. If people balked at having their privacy invaded by legislation like the Patriot Act, perhaps they could be made fearful through references to the day we were attacked on American soil and effectively silenced. If people were angry over the loss of jobs, perhaps they could be satisfied with an explanation of the attack's impact on the economy. The Republicans had a lot riding on *September 11th* going into the 2004 elections and many Republican candidates evoked the term throughout their campaigns:

"*September the 11th* changed how America must look at the world. And since that day, our nation has been on a multi-prong strategy to keep our country safer....In Iraq, we saw a threat, we realized after *September the 11th*, we must take threats seriously, before they fully materialize." -George Bush, September 30th, 2004

"The awful events of *September 11*, 2001 declared a war we were vaguely aware of, but hadn't really comprehended how near the threat was, and how terrible were the plans of our enemies.... It's a big thing this war.... It's a fight between right and wrong, good and evil." -John McCain, August 30th, 2004

"We were attacked on *9/11*. This country was attacked; 3000 people were incinerated. We have an enemy that, if they could kill 300,000 or 3 million, would have no remorse. I think it takes strong, bold action. I think that's what the president did, and I support that action." -Peter Coors, October 10th, 2004

Republicans clearly saw the benefit of using *September 11th* in their election rhetoric. One of the most concerning rhetorical moves they made with the term was to subtly connect the Iraq War to the attack on September 11th. The public's emotional response to the term *September 11th* enabled Republicans to justify particular military actions despite the fact that no evidence existed to support such a connection. The use of *September 11th* also *encouraged conformity* by implying that anyone who was against the war was willing to let our country be attacked again. In essence, Americans were *expected to understand the vocabulary of the term September 11th*. Those who *did not respond appropriately were punished.*

Even after the election, Republicans evoked the term frequently, hoping that it would continue to benefit them politically. As President Bush faced a wave of criticism regarding the government's response to Hurricane Katrina, he used the 4th anniversary of the attack to draw parallels between the two events:

"As night fell on America on *September the 11th*, 2001, we felt grief and great sorrow. Yet we also saw that, while the terrorists could kill the innocent, they could not defeat the spirit of our nation. The despair and tragedy of that day were overcome by displays of selflessness, courage, and compassion…. Today, America is confronting another disaster that has caused destruction and loss of life. This time the devastation resulted not from the malice of evil men, but from the fury of water and wind…. Once more our hearts ache for our fellow citizens, and many are left with questions about the future. Yet we are again being reminded that adversity brings out the best in the American spirit." -George Bush, September 11th, 2005

Terrorist/Terrorism

Terrorist/terrorism is the third political term persuaders have relied on heavily in the contemporary context. *Terrorism* had political meaning earlier in its history, but was elevated to an ideograph after the September 11th tragedy. The overarching emotional response to the word *terrorism is fear.* When the average American is encouraged to believe that they might be the victims of *terrorism,* or that *terrorists* might hurt their country, they are justifiably afraid. They might also respond with anger and a willingness to use violence despite the fact that it is very difficult to say exactly what *terrorism* is.[18] In truth, it is easy to argue, as some people do, that one person's terrorist is another person's freedom fighter. And yet, Republicans used the term throughout the 2004 election in ways that assumed not only a clear definition of *terrorist* but also a definitive number of *terrorists* that could be destroyed:

"This is not going to be easy. These are *terrorists.* These are people who think nothing of butchering and slaughtering their own people. The United States, I think as the leader of the free world, has to stay strong. We have to stay resolute. We need to finish the job. If we don't, the terrorists are going to prevail and I think that

---

[18] UN Member States have yet to agree upon a definition despite having tried for over 75 years. (http://www.unodc.org/unodc/terrorism_definitions.html)

spells disaster for the people of United States and for national security as we move forward from here." -John Thune, September 19th, 2004

"On September 20, 2001, President Bush stood before a joint session of Congress, a still grieving and shocked nation, and a confused world and he changed the direction of our ship of state. He dedicated America under his leadership to destroying global *terrorism*. The President announced the Bush Doctrine when he said: 'Our war on terror begins with Al Qaeda, but it does not end there. It will not end until every *terrorist* group of global reach has been found, stopped and defeated. 'Either you are with us or you are with the *terrorists*.' And since September 11th President Bush has remained rock solid." -Rudolph Giuliani, August 30th, 2004

Essentially, Republicans used the term *terrorist* as part of their larger strategy to instill fear in the American people. As the previous examples demonstrate, they often combined *September 11th* and *terrorism* when discussing the Iraq War. They made people fearful and then attempted to fulfill the resulting need for security by offering Republican candidates who would be tough and unwavering in the fight against *terrorism*. *Tough on terrorism*

On another front, the threat of terrorism was used to justify controversial legislation like the Patriot Act which arguably restricts the freedom Americans so cherish. In the second Presidential debate in 2004, President Bush artfully used the concept of *terrorism* and subtly reminded the audience of the attack on *September 11th* in order to justify the need for the Patriot Act:

"The Patriot Act is necessary, for example, because parts of the FBI couldn't talk to each other. The intelligence-gathering and the law-enforcement arms of the FBI just couldn't share intelligence under the old law. And that didn't make any sense. Our law enforcement must have every tool necessary to find and

disrupt terrorists at home and abroad before they hurt us again."
-George Bush, October 8th, 2004

In both cases the terms *terrorism/terrorists* directed the audience's behavior in ways that encouraged them to acquiesce. Though the actual case for war as a response to terrorism is a weak one, the emotions which the terms themselves elicited made it unnecessary to fully make the case to the American people. Because the term *operated at a high level of abstraction*, it made *it difficult for people to agree on its meaning*, thereby allowing the Administration to set its own course of action as a legitimate solution. If Americans had been encouraged to reason through the possible meanings of *terrorist*, they might have recognized that a military effort in the region would not yield the desired results, as the war on terrorism can never truly be won.

Better Persuasion: 3 Things You Can Do

1) Utilize *freedom* in broad ways.

Democrats are well poised to take ownership of this critical term. For one, the Republicans have overplayed their relationship to *freedom* by constantly associating it with the War on Terror and more specifically the Iraq War. As these ventures continue to go awry, they will have more and more difficulty talking about freedom. In addition, if there is growing evidence that the Supreme Court, Congress, and state legislatures are moving to restrict people's lives in various ways, the Republicans will also lose ground with the cultural value of freedom. The Democrats, on the other hand, will be in a good position to argue for freedoms including:

- Freedom from unwarranted surveillance
- Freedom and economic stability for low-income Americans
- Freedom of speech

2) Use the term *terrorist* to problematize the war and our expectations of success.

Progressives can call attention to the fact that the very ambiguity of these terms makes it unlikely that we will ever "win" the war. If we cannot win, we must begin assessing how we will withdraw. If we continue to highlight the ambiguity of the term we can slowly build the case that no definitive end can ever be achieved. Here are a series of questions you might ask:

- Do you think we will ever win the war against terrorism as we are fighting it now?
- Do you think there are a specific number of terrorists we can find and destroy?
- If a country bombed your house or killed a family member, would you be more likely to fight against that country?
- Could it be the case that the longer we are in the region and the more we bomb and kill (even inadvertently) civilians, the more terrorist groups we will create?

3) Look for opportunities to use the terms *justice* and *equal opportunity*.

It is important to remember that just as there are cultural beliefs and values that align more closely with Democratic rhetoric and policies, there are ideographs that embody our perspectives as well. The Republicans have done a good job of foregrounding their ideas and we have allowed them to backdrop our own without much of a fight. In the next few years, Democrats need to articulate our positions from our own set of values. Using ideographs like *justice* and *equal opportunity* will strengthen our arguments, build adherence, and challenge the assumptions Republican policies have been resting upon for the past several decades. Every Democrat can spread the word by writing letters

147

to the editor that focus on these key concepts. Some possible themes include:

- "This country was founded on the principles of fairness, of justice – when one person gets ahead at the expense of lots of other Americans we are drifting from these fundamental principles."
- "Everyone wants to live the American Dream and our society should let everyone have their fair shot at it. If we don't create the fertile ground of equal opportunity, the gap between the haves and have not's in this country will continue to widen and the despair of the average American worker will deepen."

CHAPTER 10

CAPTURE THE FLAG
AND OTHER SYMBOL GAMES

We live in an increasingly visual culture where symbols are all around us. These symbols convey meaning quickly, standing in for a whole host of concepts and objects that would take much longer to describe. In addition, symbols often embody values and beliefs that motivate us but which we would find difficult to fully explain. This chapter will focus on the persuasive power of one aspect of this visual culture—icons. Some easily recognized icons in American life include various corporate logos, the Statue of Liberty, and the Bald Eagle. Icons are powerful not only because they allow people to talk about intangible things, but also because they link ideas and create a wide variety of relationships that generate new ways of looking at the world.

Persuaders find icons valuable for a number of reasons. First, they thrive on their ambiguity. To an even greater extent than particular words, icons mean different things to different people at different times. This makes them very versatile. Second, icons can convey a message quickly and simply. This is one of the reasons organizations take their logos so seriously. They know that in a cluttered environment, they need to represent themselves efficiently. Third, icons often impact us emotionally rather than logically, getting us to act more quickly. As suggested in earlier chapters, appealing to emotions elicits faster, stronger, and less critically analyzed responses. Finally, as they are easily repeated, icons build a sense of connection and identification. Because we become conditioned to seeing icons in our everyday environment, we experience a sense of familiarity when we recognize them.

Icons can be even more valuable to persuaders who use them in a political context because these symbols play a large part in what America is and what it means to be an American. Icons can stand in for our history, our culture, and our values. The honoring of specific icons also provides our society with ritual and public displays of shared activities. Both figuratively and literally, they act to weave the nation together, their ambiguity allowing very different Americans to unite around them. In so doing, these icons are capable of moving multitudes of Americans. Persuaders use them, as they use ideographs, to get people to go along, to win their support, and discourage their opposition. Because there are relatively few of these symbols, they are incredibly powerful in political persuasion and the site of important political contestation. In the current context, two such symbols are the American Flag and the yellow ribbon.

The American Flag

Clearly, the American flag is our nation's most well-known icon. The flag's mythic history, from its fabled history, to its storied stand during America's first wars, to the addition of new stars as the country grew, makes it the primary image of American identity. Even as our country has changed dramatically, Americans still identify with this icon. The American flag is found throughout our society, in classrooms, on postage stamps, and in many front yards. As the central symbol of the nation, it is often used to encourage, display, and reinforce a sense of national unity. When an American stands up and places his hand over his heart to recite the Pledge of Allegiance, he often feels a mingled sense of belonging and pride. That person literally joins together with their fellow Americans in a ritual act that bonds them with one another and honors the country they are a part of. While the flag acts as the central icon for most nations, the reverence for the flag seems particularly strong in the United States. As a result, many Americans see protecting the flag and protecting the nation as one and the same thing.

150

Given the flag's symbolism throughout America, it should come as no surprise that during times of war the flag, as national icon, takes center stage. Historically, the flag has appeared in many of our most well-known images of war from its proud waving during the American Revolution, to its enduring presence in the landscape of destruction following the World Trade Center bombings. The symbol plays such a key role during wartime because it embodies who we are, what we stand for, and ultimately what we are fighting for. It also provides a sense of belonging and security. While we may be deep in the midst of war's uncertainty, we can seek haven and purpose in the icon of the flag which symbolizes our national identity. It is this same connection that elicits our feels of duty to fight for our side and protect what America stands for. In sum, we express our duty to the country by pledging our allegiance to the flag.

Following September 11th, the flag was prominently displayed all over the nation from front porches to bumper stickers. The events in New York City and elsewhere brought the American flag to the forefront of our visually cluttered culture for several reasons. First, the American flag became a rallying point and a way of demonstrating support for the country. This was an important function following the attack because we needed something which could signal our unity, our commitment, and our resilience. In addition, the media presented images of American flags over and over again in their coverage of the disaster. Some of the most memorable images include the planting of our flag in the WTC rubble, the CNN image of the fireman carrying an American flag, and images of anti-American Arabs burning the flag. Finally, most Americans felt helpless after the attacks. Everyone wanted to do something, but they were uncertain about what that something was. So, many people bought and displayed an American flag. With this symbolic act, they tried to replace a sense of helplessness with one of purpose.

While gravitating towards the flag was a natural impulse in the days following the attack, over time political persuaders used the American flag in much more intentional and strategic ways. Many politicians prominently displayed the flag on their lapels and in the background at various press briefings. Almost over night the flag was coupled with the phrase: *United We Stand* suggesting that dissent was considered un-American and would not be tolerated. The flag was also used by political figures seeking support for the decision to go to war. For example, in Bush's 2002 State of the Union Address he said:

"The American flag flies again over our embassy in Kabul. Terrorists who once occupied Afghanistan now occupy cells at Guantanamo Bay. And terrorist leaders who urged followers to sacrifice their lives are running for their own." -George Bush, January 29th, 2002

During the 2004 election, it became quite clear that the Republicans had established themselves as the Party associated with this powerful national icon. Of course, both parties still referenced the flag, politicians from both sides displayed the symbol prominently in their ads, and both sides worked to have the flag evoke a sense of pride and belonging. At the Republican National Convention as well as the Democratic National Convention, for example, the flag was evoked to signal these strong emotions:

"I was born in Europe….and I've traveled all over the world. I can tell you that there is no place, no country, more compassionate, more generous, more accepting, and more welcoming than the United States of America. As long as I live, I will never forget that day 21 years ago when I raised my hand and took the oath of citizenship. Do you know how proud I was? I was so proud that I walked around with an American flag around my shoulders all day long." -Arnold Schwarzenegger, August 31st, 2004

"John Kerry was in the Navy and so was my father. I grew up traveling around the world, living on Navy bases. But I always

152

knew I was home when I saw the American flag." -Elizabeth Edwards, July 28th, 2004

While both parties tried to associate themselves with this powerful icon, many Americans found the Republicans' claim to the flag more convincing. This was partially because the Republicans were in power at the time of the flag's revitalization. Given the context, Democrats were forced to play catch up. But the ability of the Republicans to claim the flag also rested upon the public's perception of the Democrats' relationship with our national icon. Many Americans point to instances where Democrats appeared to turn their nose up to the flag or rejecting it outright. They note that the last several times the American flag was on center stage, the public watched the Democrats defend flag burning and challenge the Pledge of Allegiance. In both cases, Democrats were associated with a position that reduced the flag's authority. In addition, Republicans have done a good job of pinning antimilitarism on the Democrats which many Americans translate into an unwillingness to protect the nation and therefore the flag.

As a result of the Republicans' persistence, and our silence, Democrats have reduced their claim on our national icon. Evidence of this loss abounds. It can be easily demonstrated in the answer to a simple question: When you see a flag flying at a neighbor's house or on the bumper of the car in front of you, which Party do you assume that person belongs to? Your answer is powerful. Some Democrats might argue that the best way to challenge that assumption is to place an American flag on the back of your car alongside a progressive bumper sticker. While such an action should be applauded, it is a defensive move and underscores our loss of this important national symbol.

Yellow Ribbons

A more recent icon to appear in American culture is the yellow ribbon. These days, the ribbon is most commonly found in the

Dub - the song!

form of a magnetic piece on the back of cars, although it is also displayed on T-shirts and other paraphernalia. While the ribbon's history is not completely known, it is widely associated with the tradition of tying a yellow ribbon around a tree if a family was waiting for a member to return from war. Its reappearance in the early 1990s, prior to the first Gulf War, was said to be in response to the ill-treatment some American vets received when they returned from fighting the unpopular Vietnam War. Afraid that a similar response would follow Operation Desert Storm, many people showed their support by displaying a ribbon while the war was still raging.

In the contemporary political context, the use of the yellow ribbon has become much more controversial. This is primarily because of the symbol's coupling with phrases such as: *Freedom Isn't Free, Support Our Troops, God Bless America,* and *United We Stand.* While some people who display the ribbons have no partisan intentions, many others use the ribbons to subtly suggest adherence to the Bush Administration and particularly the decision to go to war in the Middle East. As a result of consistently pairing these messages with the yellow (and sometimes red, white, and blue) ribbon, most Americans have come to see the symbol not only as support for the troops, but also support for the Republican Party. In essence, the ribbon supports arguments that say support for the troops means no dissent to our foreign policy. Once again, it is the ambiguity of the icon and the ambiguity of the accompanying phrases which allows the Republican Party to frame this symbol in their own terms.

In response to the Republicans' claim on yellow ribbons, Democrats have taken two approaches. First, they have opted to display other icons such as the rainbow, the raised fist, and the peace symbol. While these icons might represent a subculture that an individual Progressive is committed to, they do not effectively stand in as a national icon. In fact, each one of the symbols represents a subculture that the many Americans do not identify with and therefore quickly rejects. Most Americans

154

associate the rainbow with gay and lesbian issues, the raised fist with revolution, and the peace symbol with the hippie generation. While all Progressives should be proud to display these icons, they are ineffective at bridging the divide between Progressives and the Americans we are trying to win over.

The second response is to challenge the assumptions tied to the yellow ribbon by displaying a yellow ribbon with a different slogan such as *Support Our Troops – Bring Them Home*. This approach is generally more effective, both by utilizing an icon which is familiar to the average American, and disrupting their assumptions regarding what that ribbon stands for.

While there are creative things that Democrats can do in response to the Republicans' claims on our national icons, it is alarming to note that we have lost so much ground. When the average American thinks of the symbols, they think of American identity. When they subconsciously associate American identity with the Republican Party, rather than in a nonpartisan way or in terms of the Democratic Party, we are at a strong disadvantage that will be very difficult to rectify.

The same is true for the Republicans' claim on our nation's primary religious symbols. While the symbols do not have the wide cultural appeal of the flag and the ribbon, they are powerful representations for one of our nation's major religious subcultures – Christians. When Christians automatically associate Republicans with those symbols, Progressives lose the ability to effectively resonate with that important voting block. Some of the key Christian symbols effectively held by the Republicans include the cross and the Ichthus fish. We need to intentionally and strategically reclaim all of these symbols.

Better Persuasion: 3 Things You Can Do[19]

---

[19] While it's not something any one person can do, Progressives in the Democratic Party should work on creating and promoting a new symbol which highlights our priorities—essentially updating the party's branding through a recognizable symbol.

1)   Fight hard to get the flag back.

We cannot allow the Republicans to claim the flag as their own symbolic property. At the very least, we need to ensure that it is returned to a national nonpartisan symbol. Every Progressive should actively find ways to display their pride in their country and their flag. As we begin to take the flag back, we will need to make an obvious connection between our politics and this national icon. One thing you can do is create your own bumper sticker which includes the flag and a progressive value you associate with it. For example:

- Image of the flag/ Freedom of Speech
- Image of the flag/ End Poverty
- Image of the flag/ Progressives Want Moral Leadership

2) Challenge the meaning of *Support Our Troops* and the yellow ribbon.

At the national level, the Democratic Party needs to begin coordinating statewide efforts in which specific days are chosen for Progressives all over the country to make strong visible statements with recognizable symbols. Even without direction from the national Party, however, every Progressives can purchase a yellow ribbon which offers a different explanation for *Support Our Troops* than adherence to the Bush administration's policy. The key is to make the additional statement large enough for people to read. Some examples are already being displayed, but you can develop your own:

- Support Our Troops – Bring Them Home
- Support Our Troops – Pay Veterans Benefits
- Support Our Troops – Pay Them A Living Wage

3) If you are a Progressive and a Christian–Display it.

Progressive Christians should couple Christian symbols like the cross and the Christian fish with Progressive messages whenever possible. Americans, Christian and non-Christian alike, need to know that the Republicans do not own Christianity. In fact, the priorities highlighted in the Democratic platform are much more in line with the teachings found in the New Testament than those associated with the Republican Party.

As a Progressive Christian, you can reclaim key Christian symbols by:

- Combining a Christian fish and a Progressive bumper sticker on the back of your car.
- Creating a banner which includes a cross to use at Progressive rallies and demonstrations.
- Making T-shirts for members of your congregation which display a Bible quote in line with Progressive values and include prominent Christian icons.

CONCLUSION

ONWARD

Having completed this handbook, you are ready to participate in the Progressive's rhetorical revolution! While the various examples cited here highlight the persuasive appeals of political figures, the tools covered by this handbook are available to anyone willing to work with them. Only a handful of Progressives will actually run for office, but millions of us have the opportunity to make a difference in other ways. Every Progressive needs to think about the role of language as we chart our own course in creating political change. If we are going to win back many of the Americans we have lost, we are going to have to think, talk, and (in some cases) act differently.

In learning more about the power of language from this handbook, you probably noticed some key themes that should be remembered as you take your lessons to the field. First, good persuaders analyze their audience and the context in which they are speaking before they craft their appeal. It is impossible to build an effective persuasive message if you think only of what *you* want to say. The stories you will tell, the values you will reference, and even the language choices you will make, should reflect prior audience analysis. And remember, in analyzing the culture, values, and motivations of your fellow Americans, Progressives must listen, rather than judge and dismiss. For too long we have practiced an elitism which has distanced us from the very people we claim to be fighting for. In the same vein, we must be strategic enough to assess the context, taking the time to really know our positions so we can articulate them consistently and confidently when the right opportunity emerges.

Second, the importance of what is shared among us (common ground, common knowledge, shared cultural values, the taken for granted, Level One frames) lies at the heart of persuasion. This concept appears in many areas of this handbook including discussions on reasoning, narrative, framing, and language devices. Effective persuaders are much more interested in what Americans have in common than what makes us different from one another. While the Democratic Party, by its own admission, has at times been nothing more than a loose assembly of interest groups, we will need to better articulate our shared values and visions in order to empower the Party and reclaim the average American. A key ingredient in achieving future rhetorical success is knowledge of the contemporary common ground of our fellow Americans. Once we have been honest in that assessment, we will need to work in consistent ways to challenge and then recreate those widely held assumptions that are holding us back.

Third, in the current context, Progressives need to find innovative ways to challenge and disrupt the now taken-for-granted notions crafted by the Republicans. We have the harder job of weakening existing societal assumptions, while at the same time fostering new ones. Every Progressive needs to become more creative and braver. Follow the suggestions at the end of each chapter and think of some of your own. Consider making signs promoting our values and standing alone in well-trafficked areas once a month. Your solitary appearance will stand out and draw attention. Make fliers about important local issues and put them on cars at the mall, or start a local blog to exchange ideas. We must overcome our hesitation.

And finally, we must be in this for the long haul. Our goal is not limited to finding better messages. We must be committed to the reorientation of our society at a fundamental level. Reemerging as a leading societal voice in this nation is a long-term endeavor, a deep process engaged in at all levels from the DNC to individual Progressives. We must be willing to be patient and steadfast. Our success will not happen overnight. It is sobering to remember that the Republicans began their work 25 years ago.

There is no doubt that our task is not an easy one. But Progressives can learn a few things from the Republicans' success:

1) While your base should be kept strong, your persuasive appeals should target Americans in terms of what they hold in common. This will impact all aspects of a campaign from messaging to the candidates you select.

2) It is important to think long term—devoting resources to audience research, as well as message creation and dissemination. We need to recognize that as we change the foundational assumptions of the culture, our work will be made easier.

3) Most importantly, and perhaps most difficult, we must be disciplined in our approach. While each Progressive will craft her own persuasive techniques and pursue various appeals, there must be coherence and repetition. Together, and with leadership from the Party, we must articulate our messages in both a consistent and a persistent manner. We are going to have to put aside our distaste for hierarchy and authority, and allow ourselves to be part of something that others may be leading.

Just as we advance our own messages, we must be diligent in challenging those messages that hurt us. This must be done on two levels. First, each of us must be very aware of the assumptions held by people in our audience. We must work to disrupt the taken for granted notions Republicans have so successfully planted in the minds of average Americans by asking questions, challenging them directly, and articulating points of opposition which also resonate in the American culture. Second, we must directly challenge messages constructed and disseminated by Conservatives. For too long, we have been responding to their agenda and thoughtlessly using their language. Our inattention has cost us greatly and must be replaced with strict strategy.

160

Conclusion: Onward

With these lessons in mind, each of us needs to be actively engaged. While this handbook offers an understanding of persuasive tools, if you read it and set it aside saying "that was interesting," the book will have failed to serve its purpose. *The Progressive's Pocketbook of Persuasion* is a tool in and of itself. Everyone who picks it up should use it to improve their persuasive techniques. Try out at least 1 of the 3 suggestions for better persuasion at the end of each chapter. Get out a paper and pen to write down some of your own thoughts. Test your messages on people who are not very politically active. Pass a copy of the book on to other Progressives. Try your hand at writing a letter to the editor with your new found persuasive tools. Make your own bumper sticker, T-shirt, or button. Use this book and let it serve its purpose. Play your part in our rhetorical revolution!

BIBLIOGRAPHY

Blair, Tony. Press Conference, 20 Nov 2003.

Borchers, Timothy A. Persuasion in the Media Age. Boston: McGraw Hill, 2002.

Blake, William. The Marriage of Heaven and Hell.

Bush, George W. Address to a joint session of Congress and the American people. United States' Capitol, Washington D.C. 20 Sept 2001.

---. President Bush: "No Nation Can Be Neutral in This Conflict: Remarks by the President To the Warsaw Conference on Combating Terrorism. 6 Nov 2001.

---. President Bush Outlines Iraqi Threat. Cincinnati Union Terminal, Cincinnati. 7 Oct 2002.

---. President Discusses War on Terror at National Endowment for Democracy. Ronald Reagan Building and International Trade Center, Washington, D.C. Oct 6, 2005.

---. President's National Radio Address. 11 Sept 2005.

---. Speech on Iraq. 18 March 2003.

---. State of the Union Address. United States Capitol, Washington D.C. 29 Jan 2002.

Bush, George W. and John Kerry. The First Bush-Kerry Presidential Debate. Moderated by Jim Lehrer. Miami Convocation Center, Coral Gables. 30 Sept 2004.

---. The Second Bush-Kerry Presidential Debate. Moderated by Charles Gibson. Field House, St. Louis. 8 Oct 2004.

---. The Third Bush-Kerry Presidential Debate. Moderated by Bob Schieffer. Arizona State University, Tempe. 13 Oct 2004.

Burke, Kenneth. A Rhetoric of Motives. Berkeley: University of California Press, 1969.

Carson, Brad, with Tom Coburn, Ron Brownstein, Kate O'Beirne, and Roger Simon. Interview. By Tim Russert. Meet The Press. NBC. 3 Oct 2004.

Castor, Betty and Mel Martinez. Florida Senatorial Debate. 18 Oct 2004.

Cheney, Dick. Reception for Senator Jim Bunning. Florence, Kentucky. 12 March 2004.

---. Remarks by the Vice President at the Ronald Reagan Presidential Library and Museum. Ronald Reagan Presidential Library and Museum, Simi Valley. 17 March 2004.

---. Vice President's Remarks on the War on Terror at AEI. Washington, D.C. July 24, 2003.

---. Vice President Speaks at VFW 103rd National Convention. Nashville. 26 Aug 2002.

Cheney, Dick and John Edwards. The Cheney-Edwards Vice-Presidential Debate. Moderated by Gwen Ifill. Veale Center, Cleveland. 5 Oct 2004.

Cheney, Dick and Lynne V. Cheney. Vice President and Mrs. Cheney's Remarks and Q&A at a Town Hall Meeting. Embassy Suites Hotel, Des Moines. September 7, 2004.

Bibliography

Clark, Patricia. Press Briefing. 22 March 2002.

Clark, Wesley. Speech at The University of South Carolina, 6 November 2003.

Clinton, Bill, George H. Bush and Ross Perot. First Presidential Debate. Moderated by Jim Lehrer. Field House, St. Louis. 11 Oct 1992.

Clinton, Bill. Radio Address. 27 Jan 1996.

"Colorado Senator Ken Salazar." On The Issues: Every Political Leader on Every Issue. 5 Dec 2005. <http://www.issues2000.org/Senate/Ken_Salazar.htm>.

"Colorado Senator Pete Coors." On The Issues: Every Political Leader on Every Issue. 5 Dec 2005. <http://www.issues2000.org/Senate/Pete_Coors.htm>.

Cooper, Marc. "Is the Terminator In Free-Fall?" The Nation. 12 Oct 2005. 20 Nov 2005. <http://www.thenation.com/doc/20051031/cooper>.

Coors, Pete and Ken Salazar. Debate. 10 Oct. 2004.

Cumings, Elijah. Black Caucus. Washington D.C. 8 Oct. 2003.

Darsey, James Francis. The Prophetic Tradition and Radical Rhetoric in America. New York: New York University Press, 1997.

Daschle, Tom and John Thune. Debate. Moderated by Tim Russert. Meet The Press. NBC. 19 September 2004.

Bibliography

Data from U.S. Bureau of Labor Statistics. "Labor Force Statistics from the Current Population Survey: Annual Average Tables from the January 2000 Issue of Employment and Earnings."

Dean, Howard. Interview with Tim Russert. <u>Meet The Press</u>. NBC. 22 May 2005.

DeFazio, Peter. Press Release. 8 February 2001

D'Souza, Dinesh. <u>Letters to a Young Conservative</u>. United States of America: Basic Books, 2005.

Earl of Comarty qtd. in Fletcher, Andrew. <u>Works—Letters to the Marquis of Montrose</u>. 266.

Edwards, John. Interview with Alan Colmes. <u>Hannity & Colmes</u>. FOX News. 30 March 2005.

---. Remarks at Democratic National Convention. FleetCenter, Boston. 28 July 2004.

Enzi, Michael. "Remarks on Senate Veterans and All World War II Veterans." 2 June 2004.

Fisher, Walter. "Narration as a human communication paradigm: The case of public moral argument." <u>Communication Monographs</u> 51 (1984): 1-22.

---. "The narrative paradigm: In the beginning." <u>Journal of Communication</u> 35 (1985): 74-89.

Florida Times Union, "First Coast Area Voter Guide." <http://www.vgt2004.org/a-jacksonville/ candidate-detail.go>.

Bibliography

Frank, Thomas. <u>What's The Matter with Kansas?: How Conservatives Won the Heart of America</u>. New York : Metropolitan/Owl Book, 2005.

Franks, Tommy. First Centcom press conference after the commencement of the invasion 22 March 2003.

Freedman, Jonathan L., Sue Ann Wallington and Evelyn Bless. "Compliance Gaining without pressure: The effect of guilt." <u>Journal of Personality and Social Psychology</u> (7): 117-124.

Frist, Bill. 2004 Republican National Convention Address. Madison Square Garden, New York City. 31 Aug 2004.

Fuiten, Joseph. <u>Religion and Ethics Newsweekly</u>. PBS. 27 August 2004.

Gass, Robert H., and John S. Seiter. <u>Persuasion, Social Influence, and Compliance Gaining</u>. 2nd ed. Boston: Allyn and Bacon, 2003.

Giuliani, Rudolph. 2004 Republican National Convention Address. Madison Square Garden, New York City. 30 August 2004.

Hall, Brian and Kevin Murphy. "The Trouble with Stock Options." <u>Journal of Economic Perspectives</u>, 2003.

Hamilton, Mark A. and John E. Hunter Vita. "The effect of language intensity on receiver evaluations of message, source, and topic." <u>Persuasion: Advances through meta-analysis</u>. Edited by M. Allen and R.W. Preiss. Cresskill, NH: Hampton Press. 1998.

Hammond, Joshua and James Morrison. <u>The Stuff Americans Are Made Of: The Seven Cultural Forces That Define Americans—A New Framework for Quality, Productivity and Profitability</u>. New York: Macmillian, 1996.

166

Bibliography

Harris, John F. "God Gave U.S. 'What We Deserve,' Falwell Says." The Washington Post. 14 Sept 2001.

Hart, Roderick P. Modern Rhetorical Criticism. Glenview: Scott, Foresman and Company, 1990.

Institute for Policy Studies. "New CEO/Worker Pay Gap Study." <http://www.ips-dc.org/projects/execexcess2001.htm>.

Jamieson, Kathleen H. "Issue Advocacy in a Changing Discourse Environment" In W. Lane Bennett and Robert Entman (Eds.) Mediated Politics: Communication in the Future of Democracy. Cambridge University Press, 2001.

Kazin, Michael. The Populist Persuasion: An American History. New York: Basic Books, 1995.

Kerry, John. Remarks in Orlando, Florida. 2 October 2004.

Kerry, John. Remarks at Brown University. Brown University, Providence. 19 Sept 2005.

Keyes, Alan and Barack Obama. U.S. Senate debate sponsored by the League of Women Voters in Illinois. Moderated by Ron Magers. Springfield, Illinois. 21 Oct 2004.

Jewett, Robert and John Shelton Lawrence. Captain America and the Crusade against Evil: the Dilemma of Zealous Nationalism. Grand Rapids: W.B. Eerdmans, 2003.

Lakoff, George. Don't Think Of An Elephant! Know Your Values and Frame the Debate. White River Junction, VT: Chelsea Green Publishing, 2004.

---. "Metaphor and war, again." AlterNet. 18 March 2003.

Bibliography

<http://www.alternet.org/story/15414/>.

Lakoff, George and M. Johnson. <u>Metaphors We Live By</u>. Chicago: University of Chicago and Press, 1980.

Joe Lieberman and Dick Cheney. The Cheney-Lieberman Vice-Presidential Debate. Moderated by Bernard Shaw. Centre College, Danville. 5 Oct 2000.

Limbaugh, Rush. Address to House GOP Freshmen. Baltimore, Maryland. 10 December 1994.

Luntz, Frank. Interview. <u>Frontline: The Persuaders</u>. PBS. 15 Dec. 2003.

Lutz, William. <u>Doublespeak: From "Revenue Enhancement" to "Terminal Living": How Government, Business, Advertisers, and Others Use Language to Deceive You</u>. New York: Harper & Row, 1989.

Martin, Wallace. <u>Recent Theories of Narrative</u>. Ithaca: Cornell University Press, 1986.

Mahler, Jonathan. "The Soul of the New Exurb." <u>New York Times</u>. 27 March 2005.

Maslow, Abraham. "Theory of Human Motivation." <u>Psychological Review</u>. 50 (1943).

McCaffrey, Dawn and Jennifer Keys. "<u>Competitive framing</u> processes in the abortion debate: Polarization-vilification, frame saving, and frame debunking." <u>The Sociological Quarterly</u>. 41.1 (2000): 41-61.

McCain, John. 2004 Republican National Convention Address. Madison Square Garden, New York City. 30 Aug. 2004.

Bibliography

McElroy, John Harmon. American Beliefs: What Keeps a Big Country and a Diverse People United. Chicago: Ivan R. Dee, 1999.

McGee, Michael Calvin. "The 'Ideograph': A Link Between Rhetoric and Ideology." The Quarterly Journal of Speech. Volume 66, Number 1. February 1980.

McKibben, Bill. "The Christian Paradox: How a faithful nation gets Jesus wrong." Harper's Magazine. August 2005: 31-37.

Mehrabian, Albert. Silent Messages. Belmont, CA: Wadsworth, 1971.

Miller, Zell. 2004 Republican National Convention Address. Madison Square Garden, New York. 1 September 2004.

Mishel, Lawrence R. et al., The State of Working America, 2002-2003. Ithaca: Cornell University Press, 2003.

Murtha, John. Press Release. 17 November 2005.

Naylor, Larry L. American Culture: Myth and reality of a culture of diversity. Westport: Bergin and Garvey, 1998.

Newsweek Poll. Conducted by Princeton Survey Research Associates. 24-25 June 1999.

Noury, Alex J. and Natalie C. Smith. "Bye Bye American Dream." PoliticalAffairs.net. <http://politicalaffairs.net/article/view/385/1/38/>

Obama, Barack. Keynote Speech at 2004 Democratic National Convention. FleetCenter, Boston. 26 July 2004.

O'Hair, Dan, Rob Stewart, and Hannah Rubenstein. A Speaker's Guidebook, Text and Reference. 2nd ed. Boston: Bedford/St. Martin's, 2004.

Oregonians for Health Security. *The Daily Dose.* <http://www.oregoniansforhealthsecurity.org/dailydose.cfm>.

Pataki, George. 2004 Republican National Convention Address. Madison Square Garden, New York City. 2 Sept. 2004.

Popkin, Samuel L. The Reasoning Voter, Communication and Persuasion in Presidential Campaigns. Chicago: The University of Chicago Press, 1991.

Rank, Hugh. "Persuasion Analysis." Nov. 18, 2005. <http://webserve.govst.edu/pa/>. 20 Nov. 2005.

Reagan, Ronald. Farewell Speech to the Nation. 11 Jan 1989.

---. First Inaugural Address. West Front of Capitol, Washington D.C. 20 Jan 1981.

---. President's 38th News Conference. Hyatt Regency, Chicago. 12 Aug 1986.

Reich, Robert B. Reason: Why Liberals Will Win the Battle for America. New York: Vintage Books, 2005.

Reid, Harry. Response to 2005 State of the Union Address. 2 Feb 2005.

Rokeach, Milton. Beliefs, Attitudes, and Values; a Theory of Organization and Change. San Francisco: Jossey-Bass, 1968.

Rumsfeld, Donald. Testimony of U.S. Secretary of Defense Donald H. Rumsfeld before the House Armed Services

Bibliography

Committee regarding Iraq. Rayburn House Office Building, Washington, D.C. 18 September 2002.

Salazar, John. "Democratic Radio Address." 13 August 2005.

Schwarzenegger, Arnold. Remarks to Republican National Convention. Madison Square Garden, New York City. 31 Aug. 2004.

Sharlet, Jeff. "Soldiers of Christ: I. Inside America's most powerful megachurch." Harper's Magazine. May 2005: 41-54.

Spindler, George Deaborn and Louise Spindler with Henry Trueba and Melvin D. Williams. The American Cultural Dialogue and its Transmission. London: Falmer Press, 1990.

Steele, Edward D. and Charles Redding. "The American value system: Premises for persuasion." Western Speech 26 (1962): 83-91.

Tolson, Jay. Table of Contents Entry. "God and Country." U.S. News and World Report. 8 Aug. 2005: 1.

Trujillo, Nick and Leah R Ekdom. "Sportswriting and American cultural values: The 1984 Chicago Cubs." Critical Studies in Mass Communication 2 (1985): 262-281.

Van Natta Jr., Don and David Johnston. "A Nation at War: Banned weapons; U.S. Search for Illegal Arms Narrowed to About 36 Sites." New York Times. 14 April 2003.

Wallack, Lawrence. "Framing is More than Message." Rockridge Institute. March 2005. <http://www.rockridgeinstitute.org/>.

Wallis, Jim. God's Politics : Why the Right Gets It Wrong and the Left Doesn't Get It. San Francisco: Harper, 2005.

Weaver, Richard. <u>The Ethics of Rhetoric</u>. South Bend, IN.:
Regnery/Gateway, 1953.

ISBN 141209491-7